Read the sign above the door:
"It's not for everyone."

Broadcast, *The Book Lovers*

The Book Lovers
Steve Aylett

Proudly published by Snowbooks Ltd
Paperback ISBN 978-1-913525-32-3
Ebook ISBN 978-1-913525-33-0
Copyright © 2024 Steve Aylett
Cover art by Emma Barnes
Typeset by Emma Barnes in LaTeX
Steve Aylett asserts the moral right to be identified as the author of
this work. All rights reserved.
British Library Cataloguing in Publication Data.
A catalogue record for this book is available from the British Library.

Also by Steve Aylett:
    978-1-909679-83-2 Lint

1

Hidden Ink

'A book is like you and me – glued to a spine and doing its best.'

When Sophie spoke the secret phrase and was led down the corkscrew skeleton of a hidden staircase, she realised she had found fathom gold, the delicious contraband of the spirit.

And how poorly she had treated Lieutenant Lukas who had directed her here an hour ago! They had sat on a floral iron bench near the automatic bandstand in Lovelace Park and she had all but snipped him in half like a playing card. 'How goes the war?' she had asked. In the chill summer sun the candy-coloured affluent of Thousand Tower City promenaded at the approved pace to distance them promptly from their own nose steam. Flamboyantly accelerating and decelerating was forbidden; so was yelping and bounding vertically in the atmosphere. Anything could lead to scandal and everybody smiled. Some gazed into objects which looked like books but were actually mirrors.

'The natives are ungrateful. Our ballistic airframes are very effective, and quite beautiful in their way. There are rumours of new artillery based upon voltaics.' He glanced casually aside at her. 'Have you heard?'

'I have heard,' she said, 'that their land is still alive and their skin of a colour that allows us to pretend they are not quite human. While at the same time you, Frank, are purporting to be scarlet, with a yellow striped chest and' – she looked askance at his tall battle hat – 'a furry black head?' He was a handsome fellow but, wishing the world to know him as a man, he had put on a costume which made him resemble a toy.

He smiled. 'It's the uniform of my guard, Sophie – it's meant to be fierce.'

'Surely you are either fierce or you are not. Why wear this? But I admit I'm just as swayed by fashion – look at the nonsense I'm in. Am I a woman or an orchid?'

Nearby a couple ambled and posed according to the dictates of the season. They were like the clockwork newlyweds on a cake. It made her uneasy to see people acting like machines. Someone might get the idea to scrap them. Any excuse. 'Well I am a man, for all that,' Lukas was saying.

'Perhaps, Lieutenant, but I shall never know because you refuse to show me. In all the weeks of our acquaintance, you have never expressed an idea of your own. Without that you are just a manshape skinned of detail. They belittle you by telling you to die for something bigger than yourself. And what's worse, you would only be dying for them.'

Over at the tea pavilion, several swells were practicing the new fad of competitive laughter. A gentleman propped a penny farthing bicycle against a topiary cannon and stood there, seemingly wondering what he was about.

'If you were a man and got the call,' Lukas asked her, 'would you run away in fear?'

'Fear wouldn't be the decider – after all, many young men go to war in a state of abject terror.' Absently she twirled a pink parasol which housed a ten-inch retractable blade. 'Rather I would take that view which combines individuality and the larger picture – this tends to exclude the compulsion of current events.'

'Current events? It's war, woman.'

She gave him a wily look. 'Sometimes, Lieutenant Lukas, I think you're fooling me. Are you fooling me? Are you a clock pretending to be slower than it is?'

The question has been asked, *Could any exasperation equal that of Lazarus?* Sophie began to suspect that Frank was in the running. He gasped, 'In the name of god, Sophie, why did you request this meeting?'

'You're right, I've wasted time.' Reaching into a half-moon clutch she fetched out a book with a pink pearlescent cover and a knobby spine. 'You kindly gifted me this a week ago. I need to know where you found it.'

He looked vaguely away as if embarrassed. 'Oh that? A squalid little book cellar, under a looking-glass shop in Drood Street. Should I have bought you a compact?'

'No,' she laughed. 'You were good to give me this. And to dare the terrible risk!'

'Though I don't understand your passion for such things. And that place! So many words unattached to substance. Too thin for my blood.'

'Then how can you ever give your word and mean it, if words have no meaning for you? That sort of promise blossoms and withers in a moment. You know how I feel.'

'Yes, in fact I remember precisely: "The average fusilier is born as a jigsaw, happy to be put together by someone else." When you said it you seemed very happy and unable to restrain yourself. I believe you delight in rejecting me one piece at a time.'

'I'm sorry, Frank.' She stood. 'Whether you are this, or are pretending to be so, I fear we have no meaningful connection. Sadly it seems we lack the will to understand each other. It's a hard wrench I know, leaving altered parameters. I wish you had just been yourself with me. Goodbye.' She gave him a polite nod, and set off toward the street.

'You mistake me, madam!' he shouted after her. 'Reality is at every door and window!'

A ride across Tower Bridge in a kettle cab and Sophie located the mirror shop opposite Dahl's Chickens. The usual passphrase admitted her to a hidden basement beneath Robeck's Reflectives.

The bookherd leading her down the iron stairs was a sickle-faced and stark young man, but coming into view beyond him was the richest cache of ignored treasure she had ever seen. She stepped down to a hexagonal cellar surrounding her with shelved and heaped books lit by Talion lamps. Ingots of colour glinted as though she stood in the stilled drum of a child's kaleidoscope. There was a glutinous pull in her heart and mind. At that moment the cellar seemed to cradle books bound in flagskin, sharkskin, birdskin, saintskin, snakescale, starhide and sari silk. Books smuggled in from Samarkand and Zanzibar. Foreign packets of data and flavour. Taboo books of prohibited clarities. Flood-damaged books blemished differently on every page. Leechbooks and grimoires, lush as mud. Books with buckles, clasps, locks, tails and babyteeth. Books printed in seven colours, books with pictures and conversations, books with covers worn to a shine like chair seats and others whose skin was getting wrinkled. A book of keyholes, a book of beginnings, a book illustrating ominous curse medals, a book in which every word is a reminder. A book to ruin your summer, gleaming like a scarab. A book bitten down like a sandwich, a book of thorns, a book of page thirteens, a book which confides if your heart is heavy and entertains if it is light. A book written in self-defence, a book of last resort, a book written execution-style. Russian books which cough when opened and close like a rifle shot. A book so unremarkable it must have a secret. A book like the head of a sledgehammer. A book big enough to creak, with pages like geological layers. A book explicating a tarot no-one had ever seen. A book transmitted from one world to another, a book repaired by those who did not understand it, a book complicated as sixteen sisters, a book in which everything is true.

It was all promise and potential.

At the back of her throat Sophie felt the gluey ache she had first felt as a child. Shrinking from the doll-like stares of her playmates, she had devoured the books in her father's collection. In a box of sunlight by the window she tasted a vibratory honeychain of ideas confirming that human beings think and feel, a fact unacknowledged by the real people in her young life. Today her father pretended those books had never existed, home had armoured itself and people were behaving more like dolls than ever.

'Can I be of service?' asked the bookherd.

She retrieved the volume from her half-moon purse. 'A man gave me this. He acquired it here.'

'Are you returning it? Does it displease you?' He took the book and scrutinised it.

'No. It happens to be something I read when I was very small, and it struck me that this time the story is quite different.'

'*Darkle the Wise* by Hugo Carpstein! A flabbergasting feast of invented information! May I ask, have you visited a cellar before?'

'Do I look too proper? I've been to Prospero's, Syme's and the Fortsas. Nothing like this.'

'Well, those were bookshops once upon a time. This is my collection, everything I've read. I opened only a fortnight ago.'

'It's extraordinary. How on Earth did Frank know about it?'

'Your beau – a soldier wasn't he? – may be more lively than you think. The nearest I have to a military section is the zeppelin shelf over here, a boyhood interest of mine. And one or two bibles.' With thin limbs like a grasshopper, the bookherd stalked here and there in a metallic-blue swallowtail coat.

'Did you hear what I said about the book changing?'

'Yes, I'm still thinking about it. I have a hypothesis but it's preliminary and stupid. If you don't mind, I'll present a few alternatives. Sit down.'

They sat on either side of a small round table covered in arcane bric-a-brac. A green oil lamp lit the bookherd's cueball eyes. His slicked black hair seemed painted on like tar. 'To start with the obvious there's the example of Miss Landon's *Disgrace and Liberty*, a mannered romance printed in three different editions.'

'That's right, in each the heroine ends up marrying a different dullard.'

'Probably meant as a satire, but the characters' very interchangeability meant it was years before anyone noticed the prank. Then there's the tradition of fairytale books you can shake like a parcel and the story re-arranges. The phenomenon of expecting a certain word or idea and seeing it, though a different thing is in front of you. Or how the curvature of an idea might slingshot a person in the opposite direction. Also the strange circumstance that when a book is closed, opposite pages touch – sometimes entirely different scenes are pressed against each other, or characters touch a part of their future. What else... Well, we can see how dissatisfaction with scripture as given, and the conclusion that it must be in code, has led to the Maximudic practice of distilling and re-administering a text until every permutation is presented, a process lasting for eternity. The endless re-flourishing is supposed to express the daydreams of creation. No surprise we shut our eyes to such madness. In any case that system was wrecked when someone suggested that the big Word in the Beginning was a reply. It's called the Zeroth Pickle, I think.'

When it came to books the young man had the eagerness of a clever boy.

'But maybe what we have here is a forked book,' he added thoughtfully.

'Forked book? What does that mean?'

'Shelley pioneered it after someone told her they'd seen a man eating shark at a local restaurant. She placed a spinning engine at the heart of a book called *Open Fire*. From around the halfway point, different readers would perceive the story quite differently, depending on their turn of mind.'

'Isn't that true of all books?'

'This was a very deliberate mechanism. The split occurs when Inspector Veblen says these words: "And who do you think they'll believe – you or the police?" From that point on, the story can be perceived in two precisely different ways.'

'Depending on what the reader knows of the police?'

'It's a case of everything in the second half of the book being written to consistently mean two things, according to which groove the reader enters. It's very difficult to do, without getting all abstract and strange. Whichever version you perceive, you shouldn't be especially conscious of anything clever being done.'

'How does this apply to *Darkle*?'

'If *Darkle the Wise* is a forked book and you yourself have changed markedly since childhood, you might read a different version of it today, with no change to the text.'

'Most things have been clear to me from the start,' said Sophie with a rueful sadness. 'I feel certain it's the text which is changed.'

'Well, this is our copy – we need another for comparison.'

'Syme's is closest.'

'I'll go. May Saint Nonnatus clear a path through pesky parades and the Troy Fool save me from clowns.'

When he had disappeared up the metal steps she fell to browsing the cellar's cargo. Here was *Amnesia and the Match-Strike Devil*, in which a family of lighthouse cats declare independence for their small island but are not understood. She found a book of volvelles, its card dials appointing space and time. Airship manuals, a treatise on voltaics, a discourse on etherics, and Ludo Pepper's celebrated book on Grudge Equations, *This Explanation Has Come Too Late*. Sophie ran her finger clicking down the knurls of its backbone. There were other items in this strange inventory. A picture of a sneering badger in a triangular frame. An ancient unsent letter. A pilot's sextant the colour of brandy. A typing device with a tongue of paper. There were no looking-glasses.

The little round table was also cluttered with erstwhile goblin junk. Laid open next to a thing which could have been a roc egg was a copy of *The Hammertail*, the story of a captain who falls in love with a whale and pursues it, transforming his crew. She was reading one of the Captain's sea-sprayed tirades which concluded 'Blessed be the ignorance that separates our minds from an exterminating universe, men!' when the bookherd tapped down the stairs, flicking confetti off his shoulders. 'Parade on Needle Street, with Albion tanks. Syme's is as good for cultivating mushrooms as storing books. Some of those volumes are growing beards. And Syme is a crude fellow. Tried selling me Valentine's book of doggerel *The Owl Cannon*, then as I was leaving whispered into my eye "Let's pretend we're not the unremarkable details of this larger confusion, Benji." A quote perhaps?'

'Your name's Benji?'

'Jonah. Jonah Robeck. How do you do.'

'Sophie Shafto.'

'No relation I assume. I see you're looking at Bart's *Hammertail*! I find the whole Ship of Fools genre to be a wonderful conceit – so focussed, with a boundary about it. In life there are no boundaries and the fools come and go as they please in perfect chaos.'

'Oh I agree as to the chaos, but a few wise souls may come and go, surely? I confess it takes a determined effort to spot them.'

'Here's another *Darkle*,' Jonah said, producing it from his coat as they sat again at the jumbled table. 'Ah, you've spotted my roc egg. Did you know in different cultures the egg is a symbol of life, sacrifice or cure? This one's made of papier mache.'

'Shall we read aloud in turns, perhaps two pages each?'

'Agreed. And keep our minds peeled. Those forkers were like watchmakers or miniaturists, and often went mad. Everything is so precisely appointed and has to face two ways. So let's see.'

As they read from pages the colour of old rose, Sophie remembered how refreshing it had been, the first time she read it, to find a protagonist who was competent rather than sloshing around like a toy in a bathtub. How the people spent each twilight having crucial, impossible conversations. And how after a while the book cast such a spell that the characters seemed to move within a dream, their every move a miracle of meaning.

It all began normally. Darkle makes himself conspicuous to a Scythian demon described as a creature with several extra appetites, who acquires him as an indentured serf. Darkle is sent to fetch rare books of conjuration for the fiend and reads each volume himself before passing it on, gradually outstripping the demon's powers. Having learned the purple alphabet and mastery over a species of shadow called 'daunts', how to sprint through a love maze, hide things in mirrors, build a rock fire, squeeze two words together to get water, ride a marlin horse and other obscure marvels, he sets off on his own. On the road Darkle encounters ogres, strolling meddlers and invisible onions, is mobbed by bullfrogs in an enchanted bog, and visits Unfall, a land made of all the gaps between the rules of other countries. The combination of picaresque wandering and common sense creates the strangest effect. The generals of opposing armies give their men the same rousing speech, with identical motives and grievances. Later a variation of the trick occurs in a heated debate where the reader is allowed to lose track of which character is speaking, making it clear that their points apply both ways.

Jonah piped up. 'This scene with the war, where he's going back and forth between the lines and talks to the armourer:

"A holy war. Is your god so feeble then, that it needs men to defend it?"

"Feeble god, big army – feebler god, bigger army." *And he whispered close and sharp as if disclosing a saucy secret. "Our god is a mere stick man with a small head, badly drawn upon a fragile scrap of paper. Thus our army need be large, and mighty."*

*It occurred to Darkle that the next increment was to
have no god at all, but he doubted this would be allowed.
The persistence of the army under such circumstances
would give the game away.'*

'It says the same thing in my copy,' Sophie told
him. 'But see what's next – what animals are used
in the fighting?'

'Battle hogs.'

'Does it say that?'

Jonah stopped, frowning at the page. 'No. This is
talking about an animal called a pellicorn, all wings
and seashells. It's peculiar. Despite what I want the
text to say, the words are going their own way.'

'A pellicorn! I remember them being armoured
boar, and one of them, Astorack, joins Darkle in
his travels. In the copy I bought here, they become
war elephants with little wooden castles on their
backs, and now these made-up things.'

'Well, we need to know if Carpstein had different
editions printed. I happen to know where he lives,
out in the lesser towers. Let's ask him. If he's not
there we'll leave the book and a weird note.'

Sophie's stomach flipped like an omelette. 'Oh
god!'

'What's wrong? Is it an episode? Shall I fetch
salts?'

'No you idiot. Oh, *I'm* the idiot! I've quite

forgotten that this afternoon I am scheduled to be kidnapped!'

2

Donimo

The Donimo Club was ornamented with murky shields, looted antiquities and paintings of generals scabbed with medals and boiling with anger. Tobacco-coloured cornices gilded the upper walls like flung meringues. At one end of the smoking room, two captains of industry sat deep in chairs of oxblood leather and a third, slightly younger, had the strength to stand at the fireplace with drink in hand.

'Was a time you could hide behind a newspaper – I can barely hide my famous moustache behind this thing,' said the corpulent Lord Shafto, who was used to being listened to no matter what he said. At one with his chair, he raised the pamphlet to a face like hammered meat. 'Heard the latest? Atoms are jars of nothing apparently. We're made of transient specks! People have fifty new laws to endure. Clowns in Second Square, summer snow in

Third and the Verso Tower has collapsed, killing five. And news from the Transvaast front. They're dying to beat the band over there, and dripping their wounds all over our breakfast, thanks to the press. When will they fully unleash the glories we offer? What was that, Talion?'

'Voltraspective lens,' gurgled Aksel Talion, a cadaver of sharp angles, an always startled expression as though each instant had just occurred to him, and a chin like a witch's elbow. An accident at his primary power station had shrivelled him like a spider. All closed up and the surprise still on his face, his stillness terrified. Some old folk have the unfocussed look of a person who's been punched and landed in a chair. Talion had perfected this, along with the strategic addressing of himself in the third person.

'Voltraspective lens you say?' shouted Shafto. He found it amusing to translate for the desiccated man at deafening volume. 'Or my kettle cannons, come to that! But I expect our Amerikaan friend has something to say about it!'

The younger man was the sort of handsome that would normally dispel any need for thought or enterprise, but Jay Brewster had recently cut a swathe in the dynamo industry. He stood at the fireplace with a look of mild amusement, relaxed and ruddy-haired in a tailored suit of the Boston style. 'Skim to the bottom line, gentlemen. If the aboriginals are dying at the levels our advisers recommend, the books'll balance. If not, a prudent bit of bombing will solve the problem. You Albies have invested too much in money and lives not to invest more. You've got everything to play for. I can sell a lemon to a leech. But for a quick buck? Formulate an unbreathable philosophy and sell it to the standing dead. The idea that hell is hot or that evil works in the dark, these ignore the everyday – that hell is a shining city on a hill, and the devil a dull, excited crowd. A clerk in wood-panelled chambers suffocates a million.'

'We know he doesn't mean it,' Shafto bellowed, 'don't we Talion? Brewster with his peculiar galvanic spiritualism!'

'Oh, come, gentlemen, we are all well matched and suitable to our calling. We've each harnessed a force of nature. I put my money on fear as the great mover. I deal every day with accusations that denialism is some etheric charade. Meanwhile your own Professor Kelvin has proven denial delays entropy.'

'Those experiments were badly flawed. The most she demonstrated was that evasion moves energy.'

'Enough to turn a turbine. Oh, I predict denial

will illuminate this entire city. It already powers the
Thousand underground system. That's practically
crucifixion by timetable.'

Shafto refused to rise to this, though he had had
his own underground rail scheme rejected. 'It lacks
the integrity of a reciprocating engine,' he said. 'To
put it mildly, Brewster, I'm unconvinced of your
technical abilities.'

'That's me,' Brewster smiled. 'I don't know the
time, but I ring the bell. And I must say I've taken
a liking to your radicals and agitators over here.
Get enough factions charging around to grow a
story, you can distract from anything. Playing at
revolution is like shooting pool – you pretend what
you're doing is important. And look with concern
at the details. Sombre spectators will even join
in. If they really wish to defy power, they first
have to admit what you've given them. What has
been their pleasure. In the meantime those with no
power to influence truth will consume themselves
with fiction, entertaining every cell.' He raised his
glass. 'A world that drinks its own blood. Denial.
Suffocation. Long live the wall behind the wallpaper.
I mean a thousand cowards are a thousand times
more useful than one honest man. In back of it all
we know that.' He knocked back his drink.

Shafto's walrus-like whiskers seemed designed for

bluster and fulmination, and he made use of them now. 'Yes, well, such notions may be popular in the White Colony but *The Times* here warns of the dangerous classes. We luxuriate on their behalf, what else do they want? So long as they foot the bill for our blunders. Albion holds its citizens in two cupped hands, and is sometimes so pleased it applauds. I fear they're incapable of criticising what's beyond them except by an instinctual motion toward fire, revenge and mutilation. Why else would they suspend a shanty town from the eaves? Pray they ignore their true instincts, gentlemen, and stay in the rigging. It'll be exploding scullery maids next.'

'The Rook confused us all rather creatively with those crazy banknotes. But every precocious scamp is dead as surely as it was ever alive; every rebel and exception. There is a science lately formulated whereby the effect of a man can be measured. It seems that nature has a spaciousness in which we can move and experiment without harm – it's when we touch the sides that the sparks fly. Eh, Talion?'

'Our duty,' Shafto pronounced, 'is to correct nature's mistakes, Mr Brewster. We improved the grape, didn't we?'

Talion's mouth bulbed and pupped like a mudbubble. 'Aksel thinks a long series of mistakes might be a path to –'

Brewster cut in. 'I don't claim to have improved upon nature. It is simply in our nature to deny. Empires are built on it, including my homeland. The natives are all but gone from our minds.'

'Would you make an empire here in our capital, Mr Brewster? Is this why you are buying up towers in every quarter?'

'You have a thousand, gentlemen, and can spare me a handful.'

The three industrialists were now interrupted by the ugly and extended honking of a nearby wing-backed chair being scraped around to face them. Finally, its new position revealed the presence of Sir Percy Valentine. A glittering gadfly with a fritillary tail, Valentine had a perfect mania for himself and rumours of his mode of life were limited only by the public imagination. He doted upon his own legs, which were unremarkable by any standard, and clothed them in impractical silver trousers. His cuffs seemed to flower another layer every time you looked away. And now, wearing a crimson tailcoat with indecipherable gold detailing, he gazed ironically from beneath a hat like a smashed eclair. Though a pale imitation of his type, Valentine made a good straw man for the club's patrons to attack. 'Make provision for brilliance – here I am!

You covet our towers, Mr Brewster?'

'The higher the better,' smiled Brewster.

'And will you clear away the ropes and gantries of the poor, as though swiping aside a cobweb? I declare I shall never tire of the chatter of my eight favourite merchants!'

'There are three of us, Mr Valentine,' said Brewster with good humour, 'and we are rather more than merchants.'

'Ignore this poppinjay, Brewster,' said Shafto with exaggerated weariness, 'it goes without saying he plans to befuddle us all. Valentine, we have the measure of you – how does it go? "He put an apple on his head; It's no surprise I shot him dead." You think you're a hilarious interloper but we all wish you blasted to the grave. You belong more in a perfumed salon than a club where gentlemen discuss business and compare furies. Out with you!'

'Talion says you belong,' crabbed Talion with a struggle, 'at the Friends of Fred's Evasion, or what is it...'

'He means that salon The Cairo, don't you Talion? I'll bet it's swelteringly clever in there! My daughter attended one of your recitals last year, Valentine, and discussed it with the other survivors. The consensus was that you are a blowsy moron whose vapid lampoons and buccaneering walking style flatten the senses. You even dared give a bow at the end.'

'Well, in the theatre, taking a bow during applause is meant to signal that you are no fool, that your fontanelle has closed. I try to stay in that posture a full hour.'

'Oh I bet you do. I bet you do.'

'That show had a pre-angered audience and took a lot of setting up. We had to hoist my grudges in through the window. In any case I hope you're sufficiently recovered to listen to my latest lie? It's available now: "Two ducks collide above a lake; Give it a meaning for goodness sake".'

'And you put your name to this doggerel?'

'As with a penny dreadful, it is traditional to name the culprit on the cover.'

'Save poetry for the day an angel gives you the tour.'

'Perhaps surprisingly, I agree. I did it for my own personal satisfaction, but it fell into the wrong hands.'

'I hear your book *A Nil Squirrel* has been published. Is it on the mend? Can it compete against a looking-glass?'

Brewster chimed in. 'Oh, I heard that Valentine here invested in glass and came off very well. Gets 'em coming and going. Maybe he belongs here as much as we do. Do you know Mr Valentine's poetry, Talion?'

'I know how it can be alleviated.'

'Quite right,' barked Shafto. 'Well said, Talion.'

'Gone sickly like a liqueur,' added Talion.

'I believe you've said it, Talion. We see before us a bohemian loon whose arcane theories waste his sweet time and ours. Your poem "Failed Beans" brought an eerie tear to my eye, Valentine. And what you call "subterranean prawns" are actually beetles of various kinds, isn't it obvious? Call a thing by its proper name!'

Brewster's attitude of mild amusement had not wavered. 'I'm quite entertained by Mr Valentine's novelties and riddles. In my country we give such stuff away with candy. What was the one about the giraffe?'

'Easy to solve,' said Shafto. 'A giraffe whose neck goes on forever without repeating its pattern is a dead giraffe, because it can have no head sir, no bloody head! An idea that I don't find especially reassuring!'

'The question is,' grouched Talion, 'who cares if it lives. A huge giraffe. Watch out if it does, I warn you.'

'It's just a jest, Baron, a party trick. Like folding a balloon.'

'A balloon,' Talion intoned ominously, scowling into space.

'And the poem "Ellipump Avoidance" is about elephants I take it?' asked Shafto.

'Yes. "A head just this side of a soda syphon", what else could it be?'

'And the moon is "the sun's pasty imposter"?'

'Well I don't want to give it all away at once. It's like a snake charmer with a meerkat – too sudden, you see?' And Valentine began giggling quickly as if he'd only minutes to live. He was prone to unexpected shrieks and laughter, and changed his facial expressions very abruptly without transition. It could be quite alarming, and it enraged Lord Shafto.

'Don't jubilate when I'm talking to you! Time and again you appear gratified but nothing has happened! And I pray that in god's heaven we'll be given back the four minutes you took to turn that bloody chair!'

'You amuse,' added Brewster casually, 'but you're out of time, Valentine. We need a usable past. The Vivid Age? We just can't use it. Any more than we can use a book full of ideas. It's not on the agenda.'

'To put it mildly the world doesn't reflect my contribution, I admit,' said Valentine. 'I surpass nature in my fabrication. And to think one day it will all be undone! I'll be conducting one-sided negotiations with a cascade of maggots!'

'You'll hardly guess what he's about now, Talion!' Shafto guffawed. 'Talking about maggots! Because apparently he can do what he likes!'

'I have the good fortune of being ignored. I can say or do practically anything. By my reckoning I have now been wrong for five weeks without interruption. My mistakes are of the best quality. I have many sent from abroad. The scoundrel disowns wisdom received and signed for. I find received wisdom endlessly entertaining. If two puppets argue and two people watch, how many puppets?'

Brewster rolled a cigar next to his ear and it yielded nothing surprising. 'Your speculations are without profit, Mr Valentine – a bad investment.'

'Scold me if you will, Mr Brewster, but your enigmatic engine seems to run on misplaced confidence. The merits of the stunt elude me. Will it improve the vulgar explosions of our lads in uniform?'

Shafto couldn't have shouted louder if he'd stood to do it. 'Unbelievable that this fellow mocks us, when he wears such trousers! And has convulsions not of this world! Tin collars are a tired trick, Valentine, or are you so bewildered by gratifications you can no longer see beyond your own eyelashes?'

'Frankly, yes. I am detained by medicinal bliss. Aware in high style. A dirty trance full of blotting treasure. About your head, Lord Shafto, I perceive a nimbus of fantastic animals, none of them pleased to see you. And oddly enough, I myself am a leopard and have been for hours. See how sharply defined my ears have become?'

Shafto bellowed: 'I'm not paid to notice your ears, laddie, nor to entertain your blazing delusions. Leopard? Hours? Is there nothing in that skull of yours but dust and dolly mixtures?'

Valentine was known to pose, when he remembered, as a radical. 'Contrariwise, why should I admit that there is anything beyond the horizon of my own forehead? As for this war you so adore, it's too soon for the end of the world. Has every idea, every soup been expressed?'

'Such luxury ideals do not protect us when we are attacked from without,' Shafto pronounced.

'Should we work toward circumstances where no-one wishes to attack us?' said Valentine thoughtfully. 'A sort of adulthood or enlightenment? If we ceased our own invasions we might be hated less and have less to covet.'

'You propose we reduce ourselves to a kind of Greenland.'

Valentine looked slightly chastened. 'I admit it seems drastic.'

'Well we don't want a tricky war,' Shafto continued. 'Best by far a rolling engagement, like waves flowing together. Thus where does one war end and the next begin? The less curiosity, the more contentment.'

'Strange sentiment,' trilled Valentine, 'from a pioneer. I suppose a frontier becomes commonplace while its finder still believes himself intrepid. Old Father Steam! You've sat yourself into a curd, Shafto.'

'I've never claimed to imagination – only the sense to invest correctly. As for this curd I don't know what you mean, and the pink-iced pavilion you've got for a belief system makes me sick.'

'You know I really believe you'd do it, but I saw a parade on the way here and one of the war machines looked like a corner on wheels – or the cob. There, I've said it. React at once.'

'If it was down to Shafto here,' stated Brewster smoothly, 'we'd go into the next century using kettle guns and pan cannons. You're a dinosaur, Shafto, but I'm fond of dinosaurs, stuck in river silt with old dolls and trolley wheels, eh?'

'Shafto Steam and Boilers,' said Shafto slowly, 'is

thriving. I'm sunk with blessings, look at me. I'm ready for the gods!'

'Oh, come. A bubbling grunt from this one' – Brewster gestured at Talion – 'and you ask how high. You think I'm a tumbleweed but a soul with nothing invested has nothing to lose – that's velocity, chief.'

'What's a tumbleweed?'

'A sort of wicker asteroid we have out West.'

'The White Colony sounds like a tinmonger's paradise.'

'And powerful, very. Enough to kick your doddery empire off the bench.'

At this Lord Shafto seemed to be rocked by some subcutaneous cataclysm, and wrestled gasping against his chair. 'So you bit the hand that was you and became obsessed with wearing head galoshes and herding cattle! Raised on the legend of dumping a load of tea into the sea! What they don't tell you is that thousands of fish then pushed their scaly heads out of the water and said emphatically, "Thank you! Thank you for giving us some delicious tea! It is fantastic!"'

'Head galoshes?' Brewster asked with amusement, raising an eyebrow. 'Are you quite all right, Shafto?'

'A crazy fish looks the same as a sane one,' croaked Talion. 'And I'll eat it, yes I will.'

At that moment a liveried footman stepped into place beside Shafto with a silver dish bearing a ransom note.

3

Darkle the Wise

Sophie's coachman was attempting a shortcut to avoid the parade on the Machine Mile. Everyone had the same brainwave and horse-drawn carriages were solid with kettle cars and sparkers on the side streets. While Sophie seemed uninterested in the hubbub, Jonah wedged his head against the window to watch a skybarge dragging a massive flag resembling a stylized stellate wound. The street cavalcade featured hypnotic troop formations and rumbling battlewagons. A fusilier regiment accompanied an iron rocket with a ribcage and many wheels. Probably none of the spectators understood its function but they cheered anyway. Jonah couldn't isolate any specific ideas amid the noise. Five gun leviathans were sloping down the Fleet like titanic doorstops. The air stank of burnt dust.

'I get a headache when I leave town,' Jonah

complained. 'The gravity's different, or something.'

'It's the oxygen,' Sophie sighed. She had turned her handpurse inside-out to make a sort of bonnet which put her face partly in shadow. 'Anyway we won't be out very soon at this rate. What made you decide to open a book cellar?'

'I'm going on a trip soon and can't take anything with me. Actually I'd like someone to take care of my stockpile. Does it interest you?'

She seemed to be thinking about it behind a high forehead barely up to the task of containing her brain. 'I have too many commitments I'm afraid.'

'Such as being kidnapped.'

'I agreed to a little pretence for a friend. To keep a low profile for a few days.'

How could anyone forget a thing like that? Who was this woman sitting opposite, with the florid dress, a pink parasol like a closed lily, and a scarlet heart-attack mouth in a face pale as death? Apparently the daughter of a major industrialist, a book eater, but what else? She was brimming with herself. Did she know how intense she was?

She was looking at him hard. 'I often wonder,' she declared, 'whether the most interesting people are exactly what they seem, or something other. Have you read *Louderwolf*? It concerns a stately fellow whom the author repeatedly assures us has a terrible wild side like a wolf. Yet we never see it. He's as stale at the end as at the start. Arouet employs a similar strategy, but quite on purpose. He assures us that a character is an idiot and has him doing or saying a dozen intelligent things on every page.'

'And what's the aim of this strategy?'

'To make the reader feel stupid, I think.'

'I see,' Jonah said tightly. 'I had thought when you mentioned the stale man you were making a comparison.'

'I was, but not to you if that's what you mean.'

'Oh.' He looked at the brick wall beyond the carriage window. 'Well, I feel rather stale, mostly.'

She was still staring at him, leaning forward. 'Those interesting people I mentioned. The cover story, the dull mask. It's imposed from the outside, but the wearer is complicit. A sort of collaborator. They arrange it so that even you are not fighting in your corner.'

'Who are "they"?'

She didn't answer, and was soon looking drowsily out at the clogged street. By the time they got into the lesser towers he had forgotten the question.

Jonah's nervous vitality had a singular power source. The nature of sorrow is that it replenishes without fuss or fervour. It gave him the bitter strength of gunpowder tea and made him wish he were dead. Sometimes he fixed his will with such concentration upon a thing that he could tell precisely how little difference he was making. He felt the granularity of time passing. For him a notional book of a certain kind held the promise of hypervivid treasure, a rescuing nourishment. But it was as though most authors were under an enchantment whereby, setting out to tell a tale of wonder and novelty, they found themselves writing just the sort of book that had already been written. When he heard about Sophie's changed book, his first thought was that the spell had been broken.

Now the carriage was arrived at a small sugarloaf of a house, with only the hugely oversize chimney a concession to the city's signature style. At some time the stack had been painted in bands of colour in imitation of the towers' storeys, so that it looked like a giant knee sock. Sophie tapped a half-heart doorknocker and they waited in precarious sunlight.

'He may not be the full bob,' he reminded her. 'I told you that sort run screwy.'

'But he isn't that sort. We agreed the books really were –'

The door opened to reveal a grey pile of overlapping beards in which a face had been hung like a garnet.

'Hello,' said Jonah brightly.

'I disagree,' said the red-faced man. 'Why should I talk to you?'

'We'll pay,' said Sophie.

'Come in.'

Hugo Carpstein led them into a chaos of drained books and mummified furniture. On closer observation they could see he wore tweed on three of his four sides. As he fell into an armchair he was joined by an enormous black cat which lay nearby and set about ignoring them. Before Jonah and Sophie had fully sat down, he launched into an oration which answered eleven questions nobody had asked. 'The life you have been asking about has been finished for some while now, and it didn't go well. Life – who among us is prepared for such a contingency? The newborn quite rightly take offence. What outrage! By the time we regain our composure it's time to die. It's said that on their deathbed everyone wishes they'd lived more. I hope I'll be kind enough to myself to remember all the gargantuan shit that prevented it. But you'll want to hear about the writing, I suppose. Suffering from a fullness of the brain and hoping to be mistaken for a brilliant man, I set out to contrive a text which aims for the heavens, either to grasp or strike. To provide by my own lights the meaning I couldn't find. Everyone warned me against it, and they weren't wrong. I cranked the alphabet extra hard. Turned out I wasn't bad at stinging the page. The skill to contradict someone into a momentary paradise. A gift. My tales of the Adjusted Worlds did well enough at first. *City of Dogs and Velvet* had its defenders. *Realm of Fog and Cattle* took it a little too far. *Ocean of Elves and Pity* was the final insult, apparently. In those days the bodies of great creators were propped upright in glass cabinets to see what they did after death. I'm glad they bury or burn these days. The world is not a golem for us to write a meaning upon. Even the meaning we inscribe on ourselves lasts as long as the message on a birthday cake. I thought I was climbing but I was just crawling. Over sixty years. Not the slightest trace of my ambition remained – it was converted into smoke and experience. This head of mine's probably a collectors' item but how does that help me? I've got to the edge of my own body. My eyes are going bald. My teeth are ghosts. My guts are calling my bluff. My shadow still has dark hair anyway. I look forward to the day I'm reimbursed into nature. Time to throw in the bloody pen and have done with it. Next time, sensible values. That's the potted version. For more you'll have to pay more or threaten me.'

'Thank you Mr Carpstein,' said Sophie carefully, 'for the story. Hard not to feel that life is a disservice to the soul. But we're really here due to a narrative anomaly.'

'Is that what you youngsters are calling it nowadays? How did you find me anyway?'

'I was here once before,' Jonah explained. 'My father and I installed that curlicued mirror there, over the fireplace. I was probably fifteen or so. The glass book craze rather ruined his trade for him.'

'As it did mine. Remember Donne: "They in the sea being burnt, they in the burnt ship drowned." Have you read Darwin? A lot of trial and error, like our oldest towers. His detractors portray it like a fairytale frog, thrown against the wall and transformed into a man.'

'I think the frog was kissed,' Jonah ventured.

'Not in the original German. But after all that experience we're given a little mirror to peer into like a budgie, and it undoes us. Narcissus at the shore. Maybe we should go back in and evolve a little more.'

'We have found anomalies in *Darkle the Wise*, Mr Carpstein,' Sophie persisted. 'The part when he encounters the battlefield, and everything after – it's different, and maybe other things we haven't noticed. Look at it.'

Sophie gave him her book, and Carpstein frowned judiciously at the opening pages. Then he retrieved his own copy, which Jonah noticed was nicely shelved with dozens of other well-preserved Carpstein titles. A strange grandmother clock clucked back and forth. 'Here comes that headache,' Jonah muttered aside to Sophie. Really the whole thing felt unreal, like an extra episode after his conclusion. What was he doing here?

Presently, Carpstein looked up at his young visitors. 'Well, I could have sworn this book was locked tight for publication. The Red Ogre Box, I remember! Full of trouble! These big fatty slugs called undulongs, I remember them too, but the ... pellicorn? A mosquito the size of a chicken, all bladders and legs! What an odd creature! But you misled me, there are changes earlier than this. Yes, I noticed right away at the beginning, where Darkle performs his flamboyant burglary of the demon's home, it goes off differently. How I remember it, there's a window, a room carpeted in snakes, and a rigged strongbox. Tampering with the box locks the doors and drops a heavy metal shutter over the window. I opted for the obvious, the thief entering in armour so he could walk over the snakes which cushion his heavy tread, picking up the box and using it to block the falling shutter which busts the lock and so on. But in this copy you gave me, I see there are scorpions guarding the room, and he sends in some sort of mayor or local dignitary bound and gagged to stumble around and draw the poison, then ambles in and the rest is the same, except of course he uses the mayor to muffle the clang of the falling shutter. Yet here, in my personal copy which I know has not been tampered with, there is a savage house puma beneath the windowsill, roughly the size of Beulah here, and Darkle falls into the room, squashing it by accident. And soon after that there's something about a door-candle, a torch you light and the shadow it throws on the wall is a door. You have to back into it. You know, it's strange – I half-believe I considered including such a manoeuvre but thought it would be excessive. You don't want an idea burning a hole in the page. But then again why not?' He stared at a point in mid-air. Jonah noticed that the cat was studying the same spot. 'Did you ever read my story "Ladder of the Late Porosdi"?' the author asked.

'Yes, I did,' Jonah replied quizzically. Carpstein remained silent, so he continued. 'A group of honest men find a king within their power. Agreeing upon mercy, they beat and scar his face in a way that renders him unrecognizable and leave him in a remote crofter's shack in another country. Awaking there, the rogue can convince no-one of his identity, and doubts it himself.'

'Yes.' Carpstein twitched out of his reverie. 'Smart writers assume their work has no effect on the world, but it happened, perhaps for the first and only time. I've been told by those who know that Spain's King Amadeo is alive and acceptably well in Abyssinia, though he was a problem that probably would have solved itself. He's rather adored as a local eccentric. It's why I can be rather abrupt with fanatics. I apologise. As for this ... weird proliferation, it has a feel of different times, when there were possibilities. The Vivid Age! That ultrafertile everything was a long time coming, and even then it burst the window-frame. A butterfly bit my arm, if you can believe it. That's how it was then, rich and unpredictable. Nature was a welter of stimulation.'

'Was it really so wonderful?' Jonah asked. 'I was too young to remember.'

'Only twenty-so years ago, but it might as well be a thousand. I remember walking a landscape so particularised everything was a novelty. One item could be admixtured with another to make a delightful joke, a fertile idea or a droll new colour. All and nothing was at stake. The smallest act had an infinity of flavoured repercussions, and summer blew lightly through everything. As for the Troy

Jester, blessed be his name and vapourized body, he lurched through one enlightenment after another, holy with chemicals. They say he could lick his own eye like a lizard.'

'Could he?'

'Lord, no. His phosphene appetites forbade it. Then society erased him piecemeal, pretending disapproval in fear.'

'Is that what happened to the Age?' Jonah asked.

'It was fashion, I think. There's the old saying, "A true thing is best not coupled to fashion, or it may be taken away with the tide." The core of a thing can be jettisoned as the eye looks aside at something distracting. The misdirection of a conjuror. And at some level people are complicit. But a damburst of creativity now, after the vacuum? I don't know. In any case, that way lies madness. I have long grown out of the notion that every fiction exists, somewhere.'

'You're wise to think so,' Sophie told him. 'They don't. Not all, willy-nilly – that would certainly be madness. To bring a thing alive requires a plan and precise application.'

'Of what?'

'Of oneself. And of the one who receives it.'

'This sounds like a trick, or shared madness. Or complicity in a lie.'

'Or revolution,' said Sophie.

'Ah!' Carpstein nodded, and that was all.

'Well!' said Jonah briskly, trying to move things on. 'I've been "stinging the page" myself lately.'

'Any good?' the author asked.

'Too many ideas.'

'No matter. No-one will ever read it.'

'I know.'

'The grace,' Carpstein added, 'sometimes lifelong, of nobody paying attention. There's freedom.' He winked.

At the door, Jonah thought it wouldn't be a bad idea to depart with a quote from one of Carpstein's better-known works, and declared with a smirk: '"I entered entire, I exit entire. And bored."'

Carpstein gaped at him in astonished affront.

It was twilight when they left the little house. The cab was waiting, which amazed Jonah. 'Did you pay him to sit all afternoon?'

'Before I forget,' said Sophie, stopping to pull a small book from the pink folds of her gown, 'this is written by the genius who inspired my kidnapping. If you like it, meet me in the chapterhouse of Saint Dismas Chapel at noon tomorrow.'

Jonah took the volume and clenched like a star gathering itself to burst.

4

The Thousand Times

Detective Inspector Nightjar favoured the Raven Method and had received the Order of Merit for her work on the Heddon Street Outrage and a Royal Pin for the Sickert Affair. She knew that learning is the opposite of talking, that a key to a heart can kill, and that the average policeman, unburdened by repercussions, crushes clues on the way out. Liking to stay on top of the situation, a man saddles a thing to understand it, adding himself. 'Must one be a part of chaos to truly comprehend it?' Nightjar wondered. 'Isn't that the structure of a swindle or practical joke?' Possessed of a propulsive cognition, she was able to move with ease between a dozen different scales, drawing equivalents between things not immediately alike. She had come straight from the Donimo Club – alcohol, shadows and advancement – to Lord Shafto's shield-like home, the Steel Tower. Wrapped in the wings of an Inverness coat, every layer and cape black as burnt paper, she entered Shafto's state room as the Iron Walrus himself was shouting point-blank at a froglike footman. 'Take the watch, Quadfrey!' The servant disappeared through a dimpled metal door. Shafto was seated at a chrome table and behind him three round and riveted windows gave out on the tangled city. He hailed her. 'Inspector. I was told to expect you. You've a formidable reputation. You get your man and shun the warpaint.'

'Odd that women are encouraged to wear cosmetics, when it is men who resemble gargoyles.' She seated herself at the table. 'I noticed that your front door is round and turns open like the head of a giant screw.'

'The head of a giant screw, yes. Shall we get down to business? My daughter's been kidnapped by a lunatic.'

'Of course.' She flopped open her notebook. 'When did you last see her?'

'Day before yesterday. We argued about the war. She just mentioned the usual things about the dead pockets of the poor and how poverty was a gravity well even for the gifted. This to me, who built myself up from rust! I said to her if there are people like that in the world I never met them, and the last thing she said was "They make a point of avoiding you, and hate you father." What have you turned up so far?'

'The letter was bound by a gore seal, a dollop of thick arterial blood. The use of collage for the note itself implies a creative bent, a desire for anonymity or both. The city newspapers are all one so we can glean nothing psychological from the choice of raw materials, in this case the *Gazette* and *The Chiliad*. The document is stained on the edge with egg. Whoever assembled it was having his breakfast and perhaps chatting with an acquaintance or doing any number of other things. It appears to have been tossed off absently while he had other things on his mind.'

'Other things on his mind? Eating eggs? Perhaps he was throttling an emu or dancing, yes, dancing with an emu as my daughter sat bound and gagged in another room!'

'It seems unlikely. Try not to let your imagination upset you, Lord Shafto. I'd be surprised if this emu you mention has any bearing on the case. All I meant to say was the culprit is a busy fellow, with a busy mind. And then there is the style of the narrative. Odd phrasing but really every sentence is a direct hit. It rings a bell.'

The text of the note read: *Your daughter is ours.*

War's manifold misdirection moves the money with freakish grace. Stop pushing and have a rest.

'Quite clearly,' Shafto stated, 'they want Shafto Steam to stop bidding for the next push abroad. My kettle guns will be a boon against the savages. It'd be a crime not to ship 'em.'

The Inspector's eye wandered to the wall where a picture of Shafto hung framed in a locomotive wheel. It was traditional for the ruling class to portray the hams of a dynasty in sullen portraits known as 'sulk panels'. This painting and all its toasted detail depicted the magnate propped like a pig in a haunted abattoir. Near to that was an industrial-looking crucifix half a yard tall. 'Are you a Christian sir?'

'Turn a cross to the wall, it's still a cross.'

'Who else was present when the note arrived?'

'Jay Brewster, an upstart and professional bamboozier, all sham and enlargement. A cowboy who claims to generate power as near as I can tell by a sort of hydraulic seance. What next? A city driven entirely on sarcasm?'

'It's been done by the French.'

'Either way his technology is new as a pimple. The rest is charm and flummery. If he's an engineer I'm the King of Freedonia. The other man of business present was Baron Talion, who sells what he lacks.'

'Such as.'

'Energy. Vitality. Motive force. You'll be lucky to squeeze any sap out of him. He's been stretched dry by a turbine and heaven knows what seizures induced by all those galvanometers. Well, respect due him for having humbled himself before the ultimate voltage!'

'And the three of you form a sort of syndicate?'

Shafto seemed to waver, his expression smeared and grubby. 'No I wouldn't say so.'

'A cabal, then.'

'Not really.'

'A loose alliance. An informal meeting of merchant princes. A reading circle?'

'Now, now. We share comparable business interests. It is a loose coalition at best. To discuss world commerce.'

'You are in competition to supply the military.'

'Brewster's pitch is a parlour trick, we can forget that. Talion proposes voltaic munitions, a cannon that fires an electric ray. He claims his weapon operates by creating a charge imbalance which is then corrected by a sort of lightning bolt. By this logic anyone who had a need for a thing would manifest it. That's not how nature operates, in my experience. And comes to nothing having a deathray if some bleeder can nip out of the shadows and gape your throat.'

'Here in the city, or abroad? And it's said Brewster motivates the underground funicular system.'

'Well, what's he got to hide? Underground railing!'

'There's an old saying, "When you tire of the Thousand Towers, start digging downward." Who was the other gentleman present when the note arrived?'

'Oh, Sir Percy bloody Valentine. Glides around town in a Sparks Landau and won't shut up about his legs. He'll arrive all flurried and shrieking of blood in the streets, and then sit down calmly to the club supper. After which he'll start talking about starlight, jellyfish, all sorts. Says hello in the wrong part of the conversation. He's not of our group, we just look up from what we're saying and there he is, wearing silver trousers. How to deal with a man wearing those peculiar trousers? You'll die of the head staggers before you figure that one out. For sheer bloody annoyance he's second only to the street clowns. A decadent fool who means nothing he says, or less. Split the difference and call him an aristocrat.'

'Did he seem more than usually aggravated today?'

'He mentioned he was a leopard but didn't particularly insist on it. But I must say Inspector, it seems perverse to throw suspicion on those who happened to be lolling there when the letter arrived. Why not blame the waiter?'

'The waiter spent the morning knelt at a shrine in an upper room, praying to a flapjack in the shape of his mother.'

'I beg your pardon?'

'Can you tell me why the kidnapper targeted your daughter? Talion has a son, I understand, and Brewster a wife. And why would those gentlemen care?'

'Well, Sophie is well-liked – the yank and the cadaver know her, she knows them.'

'Really?'

'And I would think it quite obvious that a villainous kidnapper would select as a target the foremost steam tycoon in the greatest country in the world.'

'Of course. So obvious a thing might have been done sooner. But there are those who would argue that nomatic denial is the energy of the future, voltaics the present, and steam, frankly, the past.'

Shafto began puffing into his own mouth, his whiskers flummering. 'And what creates Talion's mysterious volts? Steam turbines! As for Brewster, I don't hold with anything that needs believing in. Talion and I tolerate the man because he invests, generously, in our joint enterprises. Shove him hard and money spurts out of his nose. I gave him a talking-to at the club and he stood there grinning like a bloody vole. No, you'll find I'm the driving force of our powerful little group.'

'A structure made entirely of rivalries isn't sound, and its details are pure distraction. You've considered of course that Brewster or Talion abducted her, hoping you would abide by the demand and eliminate yourself from the running?'

'They wouldn't dare.'

'I see. For my own curiosity, is there any actual chance of peace out there?'

'Peace? Well, I like doves but only to talk about. Carnage was a small price to pay for trade routes between India and the Cape. With Clark Dyer's airframes nothing really changed – we still need to drop anchor on several fronts without being pelted with spears.'

'I was once told an experimental proof for what is a war and what is an invasion. It's said that if you stop attacking and there is peace, it was an invasion.'

'That rather ignores the continued ill feelings of those that have been invaded.'

'Yes I suppose it does. Is this Steel Tower operational? Does it do anything?'

'Keeps the rabble out.'

'And your secrets in.'

'Secrets? Don't have any.'

'And being made of metal, it would be hard for a torch-wielding rabble to burn it down.'

'I daresay they could parboil me, with preparation. But isn't it your job to deal with revolutists?'

'The Chancellor of the Circuit keeps tabs on such histrios. I investigate crimes. Do the chess statues on the front lawn come to life?'

'Yes, they go to war at night, giggling. Shall we focus on the facts?'

'Of course. As to Sophie, is she capricious? Ungovernable? Flighty? Impetuous? Unaccommodating? Wilful?'

'She's alive and animate if that's what you mean. We don't conduct ourselves in the terms of a gossip novel.'

'Incendiary then.'

'Not within my hearing.'

'A dreamer.'

Shafto snorted. 'Can one be wilful and a dreamer?'

'Yes, I think so. Unwed at twenty-two. Quarrelsome?'

'Calm. I would say she has a serene obstinacy.'

'She sounds quite singular.'

'She is ferociously intelligent – I hope that does

not make her singular. Though in today's world...'
Shafto's voice petered out.

'In today's world, you were saying?'

'Nothing. Nothing, of course. I mean to say, I
told her, at quite a young age, "Try to use your
mind as little as possible. The heart perhaps on
occasion, but never in tandem with the mind."'

'No doubt your sage parental warning worked
like a charm,' said the Inspector with a straight face.
'It does in every case. Does she have any interesting
friends or profess any interesting ideas? Is she likely
to be bedazzled by common sense or other utopian
fancies?'

'What are you implying? That she's gone off the
rails and is secretly some kind of vamp? She's a
normal young girl. Adorns herself in the latest,
stupidest frocks and bonnets.'

'Does she have a beau?'

'Oh, there's been a fellow lately, name of Frank
Lukas.'

'Who is he?'

'In round figures, I daresay nobody. An army
swell who gads about in full dress uniform. Very
dashing and he knows it. Cavalryman I suppose, a
flakaroon. Probably a cad but what motivation
would he have for this sort of thing?'

'Oh, motivation's just a grudge with a chocolate

surround, really.' Nightjar sketched a playing card in her notebook.

'Well, fling a piece of liver at the buck, see which way he jumps.'

'Angels too are tempters, Lord Shafto. I suspect Sophie is a reader? For some people, following makes it possible to start, and the most unprepossessing philosophy can lead a fool into mayhem. Perhaps she values justice above the legal norms of the day. In a world like this it may take precocious cunning to do the right thing. I don't equate reading with intelligence, much less independent thought. Some of my colleagues can't read and are quite sharp I assure you, and many readers never have a thought of their own. But as an indicator it tells a story, like a rope around a suitcase. I see you have on that side-table a bound compendium of *The Thousand Times*. And the coverboards are made of brass. Would you preserve the words of the past, Lord Shafto? If I were to turn a hidden switch in here, would a wall slide aside to reveal a library?'

Having working himself up like a generator, Shafto seemed abruptly to chill over. 'I'd heard you were a queer bird but is this how you investigate a crime, missy? By hurling accusations at the victim?' He stood and leaned over her. 'Listen to me, Detective Inspector Nightjar of Caledonia

Tower. You may be used to staring like a great horned owl with tubular eyes until people are down on their knees explaining themselves, but I could buy eleven of you in the time it takes a crab to turn around. You'll find my daughter or I'll have you conducting cattle.'

'What a clear way you have of putting things,' Nightjar said brightly, standing and putting her notebook away. 'For some, clues appear plugged into the surface like raisins in a fruitcake. For others it's more textural, at the atomic level. That takes more time. But I will apprehend the situation, Lord Shafto. Down to the studs.'

As she pulled on her leather gloves, she gazed out at the rigged and netted spires. 'Looks like a haphazard confection doesn't it?'

Shafto did not reply.

'But I assure you it isn't.'

When she left he was standing at the fireplace, which was cold and large as a cathedral door.

§

Nightjar's notes: Expecting a square-rigged gent, I found a thing like a boiler venting surprisingly from occulted valves. He is a made man from the North who wishes to rival Rothschild's victory at Waterloo. As for the daughter, I get the impression of a contained imp radiant with mischief. Headstrong and heartfelt together. A formidable tragedy. Lord Shafto states that they quarrel about war and that she is not quarrelsome. Many's the man who found himself in hot water for sentimental reasons. Frank Lukas, rake or rebel?

5

Truth's Flying Visit

The fruiting body of a book is in the reader. Emmanuel Feste and his legendary wherewithal were well known to Jonah, but he had never heard of *Truth's Flying Visit*. It was a little jewelbox of a book with a spine as massed and detailed as a totem pole. Its waxy cover was set with an emblem raised like a seal, portraying a tower in stormy waves. The pages felt like wallpaper and smelt medicinally of cloves. There were itches between the lines of any interesting book, but this thing was a deliriant, a gem of the vindication genre, each page in collusion with every other. Its luminous geometrics were continually inversing to re-link and re-ignite, with the citric adrenal flush of an idea changing colour like a chord shift. The detail was alive with electric trickles and multifoiling filaments.

It began: *When infinite, why bother with a face? The urge to fixed order results in a history of stops*

*and lurches. Like witches we are terrified of a flowing
stream. We see historic icons such as Napoleon in a
stance, ambered in significance. In fact they were all
skidding around like dogs.*

And ended: *As for death, start without me.*

Jonah read the book bug-eyed in his hexagonal
library. Through those exploding minutes he was
feeling crossfires in his belly. Every word had the
compressed information of a seed. All his years
hoping for a typographic saint who would place a
pattern over the world which fitted just imperfectly
enough to throw bent sparks. He had felt himself
sometimes on the fluttering brink, but this slim
volume of sedition had been scrawled in some
divine frenzy, each word punch-drunk and urgent.
The delicious squinch of clarity like a blade's edge
through an apple, and something else. What was
that controlled glee which came of telling the truth
despite everything? This tirade was so confoundingly
contrary and richly appointed that one might sit
in it and be suspended. It had the particular zing
of wet electricity that went with ideas scrambling
across the brain. He felt solved and released. He
was sick with it. He was on red and black fire.

By the time he found Saint Dismas Chapel in Very
Street he had settled down into a celestially-flavoured
amazement. Votive padlocks hung loose off the

doors and Jonah entered an atmosphere of chill dust and puzzle-glass windows. The scene was completed with a picture-perfect nun in black habit, knelt at the debaser. Jonah approached her. 'Many have said "Let us finish what god started" as an entrance to cruelty. Is this your secret life?'

'Don't be silly,' Sophie said, straightening up with a smile. 'Giving your life to a church is like taking a bullet for a cauliflower. You think god lives here more than elsewhere? Split a piece of wood and I am there. Lift a stone and you will find me. Burn the knot and part the smoke, Mr Robeck. Did you read the book?'

'I ate it front to back, leaving a semi-translucent husk. There's a strange feeling in my mind.'

'That book's booby-trapped and can defend itself. You'll probably dream differently tonight.'

'In my dreams I scramble through an incoherent jumble of expectations, hopelessly compensating and playing catch-up.'

'I know,' she laughed. 'Most people do.'

Their voices echoed together. It was strange to see her big gnashy mouth in this over-arching gloom. Parliament flagstones and the smell of burnt hair. The ceiling sprawled with decorative omens, a pictorial fuss of endorsed saints jumping about in dramatic understanding.

'The dead revived,' Sophie mused. 'A good idea? Salvation is very competitive, it turns out. This one was introduced by the rite of mythical overlay, with a central rosette and riches on a Friday. Theology that seats a hundred. Careful in here. One prayer too many and you'll eject into outer space.'

'Prayer? I know you're joking. But then, only humanity's side of the correspondence has survived. Everything becomes ordinary eventually, doesn't it?'

'What if I could show you something that never will? The good sin of thinking for oneself. It's always rather immediate.'

'I think you know I do that already, and have nothing to show for it.'

'The accepted wisdom is that intelligence is near worthless or a distinct hindrance. I don't agree. Though it can't be all fun cooped up in that head of yours.'

'Sometimes it's extraordinary. But it turns bad when I run myself into a corner.'

'Without the advantage of your own soul, there's no polestar in chaos. Fortunately, some round-the-corner part of you hasn't got sick yet and never will. Look into your soul, young man.'

'I do, regularly. It's very entertaining. I happen to resemble a startled ant but I'm not without content.'

'I don't mean "content".' She narrowed her eyes and peered into his face for a while. 'Alright, come with me.'

'To see your kidnapper,' he said dryly.

'Yes.' She swooped the habit off over her head and tossed it into a corner as they left the church. 'Religion. You can't take it with you.'

Beneath the disguise she was kitted out like a street boy, her hair concealed under a battered cap – a fetish known as Lambing, after Caroline Lamb's pestering of Byron as a pageboy. Jonah accompanied this urchin onto a Sparks trolley smelling of thunderstorms and they rattled toward the Mute Quarter looking at the floor. She tilted into him on the wooden bench. 'Subterfuge rarely feels edifying,' she whispered, 'but may get things done.'

They stepped off the trolley to find Thims Street all a-mill and a-giggle with the harmless classes. A fashionable young woman indicated her own reflection in a looking-glass book, and her beau smiled approvingly at the image. Turning the wrong way between bulbous, candied shopfronts into a narrow alley, Sophie began climbing an iron escapade. Jonah stopped to ask: 'Roofland?' Getting no answer, he followed her.

Halfway up they diverted along a gangplank to a

neighbouring tower and began a jigsaw journey through the tangle of rope ladders and dangling shacks which formed the rookery. Many towers were etiolated due to each floor being smaller than the last, while others had enough roof-space for encampment. All but the most exclusive were draped in a network of cables, rigging and gangways, into which Jonah had rarely ventured. They were heading saltside and Sophie was navigating the spars and catwalks with assured ease. Jonah followed, wheezing on top of the world. The trip was a jumble of steeples, tents, belfries, suspended kennels and terrifyingly flip-flopping rope bridges. They walked down a loud ramp amid the cries of seagulls and then Sophie went over the roof edge. Jonah peered down to find a rope-ladder. Very slowly and shakily he descended to a platform which gave a fine view over the thin black beach and brown waters of the river Fleet. From here he could enter what seemed to be a shed and half a stagecoach, bandaged together in sailcloth and pitch oil. It hung lashed to the side of a dockland stackhouse. When he pushed at the door the stale wood powdered on his hand.

Jonah stood gasping in the shadows. His vision cleared the way bugs rush away when you lift a log. Two stained windows gave out onto nothing. The tilted room was half-rotten and creaking like a boat.

Sophie bustled with something he couldn't see.

At a table like a broken biscuit sat an extraordinary man tricked out as a marzipan bandmaster. He removed his purple boater and dropped it on the floor. 'Hell enters by the hat,' he muttered.

'You're Percy Valentine, the poet,' Jonah exclaimed.

'I am that.'

'Wearing a stupid beard.'

'All beards are stupid, I think you'll find,' said the man, removing his beard and tossing it on the table.

'I once grew a fair representation of a beard – I didn't dislike it especially.'

'It's easy to mistake the improvement of one's own circumstances for an improvement in the world at large. It's the replacement of a filter.'

'I don't see the correlation –'

'Eaglet, bring the eggs!' the man shouted. 'And some of that inky tar for the toast! Breakfast has worn off.'

A ragged boy wearing a dented bowler stuck with feathers entered by another door with three eggs and put a pan atop a small woodburning stove. Jonah noticed that the shack's doors had been sawn to trapeziums to comply with the slant. 'What is this place?'

'This little crimp is the Custom House,' said the

man in the humbug jacket. 'Our dicey home from home.' He flapped a hand through his mustard-coloured hair, which stood up in italics. 'Sit down before you fall down.'

'I have to change,' Sophie announced. 'Don't burst his head off his shoulders.' She left by the thin side door. Jonah sat on a cog chair stinking of Fleet water. There were pictures on the wall that had been wet and dried out. They seemed to be childish drawings of dinosaurs and a few boats. There was also a coffee-coloured photogram of Walt Whitman. The eggs started frying.

'You run a book cellar, Mr Robeck?' the man asked, regarding Jonah with frank curiosity. 'A going concern? Are enough people still reading?'

'Reading. Yes. It's beyond unfashionable but is it illegal yet, in fact? I don't know. No-one seems to know or will admit that they don't. Glass books just put the glaze on it.'

'Yes, it's quite immaculate isn't it? The eighties has got everyone looking over their shoulders, and other people's. Peer paranoia amid cultural blandness. *Something*'s been perfected here. A level of sustained skittishness that fragments thought into fluttering particles and makes everyone available to whatever the state wants of them. I don't mean to admire it, but my goodness. A salted field would hold more nourishment than this desolate show. We find ourselves in a time when we are not supposed to have any troublesome emotions or interesting ideas. What's left? A happy robot.'

'Well, I'm neither, Mr Feste.'

'Why do you call me that?'

'The books.'

'Oh, I did some of the early handbills but Sophie's your man. You've taken quite a shine to her haven't you?'

In Jonah's body, Sophie's face and heart flared open like a Catherine wheel. 'She's...' He did not have the word.

'Sophie is gold,' said the gentleman. 'From her electric head to the soles of her feet, sovereign gold. She's a drop-dead genius. Her morality has five extra gears. I didn't even start it. You're not the first to experience her strangeness in an ecstasy of details. First time I met her she was disguised as an old lady hunched as a prawn. My actual name, for these purposes, is Thomas Dollivar. How are the eggs going, scallywag?'

'There's a millipede in the pan,' said Eaglet.

'Yes we've certainly had our share of millipedes in here I daresay.'

'Did you say "share"?' Jonah exclaimed.

'Ah, Jonah, you can always eat in a neighbourhood

studded with barnacles. Straining the curtains for moisture. And starfish are surprisingly crunchy. They'll last a thoughtful afternoon. Speaking of which, a thoughtful man might wonder if life is as stupid as it is dangerous. For all you know, a moment like this was pure chance.'

'No, it's clearly been orchestrated. I can't stand it when things happen by accident.'

Eaglet placed a plate of eggs before Dollivar, who set about them. Their smell dampened that of the nearby vitriol works. 'None for you,' the renegade said. 'Fugitives are expected to have atrocious manners. And that's not entirely wrong. A hero is best appreciated when he's no longer alive to ruin it. What did you expect?'

'I expected a bristling outlaw or humourless plug of lard. A bomb-throwing Georgist with guns stashed under the floorboards or something.'

'There's empty air under the floorboards, sonny. Here's my barker.' Dollivar pulled a firearm from somewhere and placed it on the table next to his plate. 'A Benko revolver with a cut barrel and a bogwood handle. I can take it anywhere and I'm a rubbish shot. Two marks of a land that's losing control. This is in my pocket the whole time I'm posing as zany at the Donimo Club and oh I have been tempted. Do you grasp the strenuous forbearance it takes to listen under heavy manners to the starved rhetoric in that place night after night?' He scarfed at his food. 'Truly, commerce has perfected repetition! What those brigands owe me in hours is beyond money to pay. Thank god I was heir to a dung fortune. If I were entirely poor and with a need for others' resources, I would have to organise – and I don't like crowds. Have you seen the local so-called anarchist factions? The Patternista, the Ignicione, the Wind-Up Benevolent Society, the Obliterati, the Salutation Committee, the National People's Gang, the Spud Syndicate and the Jugglers' Council. God help us all.'

'What's your group called?'

'I don't know, I don't think we have a name.' He called out. 'Sophie, does our group have a name?'

Her voice came through the door. 'Deserters?'

'Too hangdog.'

'The Nerve?'

'Sounds French.'

Sophie re-entered the room dressed as a coin mistress. She had mussed her black hair like a blowsabella. 'What about the Valentines,' she said, sighing wearily as she sat down. Even as a faded shopgirl she was as vivid as a new ingredient and Jonah wanted to eat the colour out of her head like sherbet.

'We do owe that fellow a lot,' Dollivar told Jonah. 'Valentine's silly sequins antagonise while giving nothing to strike at. The behavioural cues of a fool resemble very closely those of a parliamentarian. I studied those at the Donimo and found myself both accepted and dismissed as one does a gull. A spuffy spy in the enemy camp. But his lurid frivolity costs me a great effort, I assure you. Too many binary epigrams will have a fellow talking like a seesaw. And those trousers!' He finished eating and propped back, hanging his arms. 'Are you bored all of a sudden? I know you're dazed by compromise but isn't this interesting?'

'My face doesn't always cooperate with my feelings. In fact I assure you I'm having a heartboggling afternoon. Thank you.' He turned to Sophie. 'And you are the author of the works of Emmanuel Feste.'

'Don't be cross with me, Jonah. Those ideas' acidic colours entertained my blood for years. It's time they were let out.'

'That book, eh?' Dollivar pointed aside at Sophie. 'Not a normal explanation exactly, more of a pelting run through a funhouse isn't it? The average philosopher tampers with his own restraints while issuing volumes of intricate misdirection. This one deals in atmospheric transactions, loosening knots in the air and hinting twenty things at a time. The intention is then to recall the entire book in a single hit like an ideogram. A stunning arterial release.'

'It can be fun to hide something important in a big silly symbol,' Sophie said.

Eaglet took the used plate and left the room. Dollivar put his machine pistol away.

'In the tarot,' Jonah told them, remembering the cover of Sophie's book, 'there's the symbol of a tower struck by lightning and the inconvenience that follows – it represents an accident or reversal but one which has been building up rather obviously for a long time.'

'I suspect the tarot is an elaborately encoded cry for help,' said Sophie.

Dollivar agreed. 'Surely a fellow's presentiments should arise naturally, by combination of everyday impressions, and thereby give him the collywobbles out of the blue? Seeking it out at all hours is pushing the tide. Anyway a superstition ought to enliven a fellow at least, not leave him sullen.'

'When the world has had done with a person,' said Jonah, 'how does it communicate this? Every way it can. And that's a lot.'

'And a shark is just a pilchard pushed to its limit.'

'Oh, things have a way of not working out,' Jonah countered. He always talked too much when nervously excited. 'Haven't you noticed? It's in the air – the gears of it are quite visible at times. And acceptance is not the sweet leveller you might imagine. The world simply stabs in from a new angle, always adjusting and ever vigilant. My mind has three times fallen into ruin.'

'Recently?'

'The last time was at the Fawcett Air Spire where my brother's an engineer. I was studying to be a steersman at one time, and he showed me behind the scenes. It's actually frightening to see how an airship really works, how thin the floor and walls are. Subtract one element and you have chaos. Hell could be kept further at bay but that would be too expensive. And so everything is put at risk repeatedly amid the stink of creosote. I can't even ride on them now.'

And it wasn't all that. In the air a zeppelin pilot was heroic with purpose. On the ground he walked badly and gazed up at dirigibles drifting sadly like lost whales.

'When I find a situation threatening,' drawled Dollivar, 'I use it to breaking and move on. Fearful living makes a soul quite sick. If you're real you're at least equal to a potato, lad. Have a little grit.'

'To what end.'

'To make good on the blue sky. And the grey.

Call everything's bluff, my friend. Convert shelved defiance to accurate action. You think action is crass?'

'No,' said Jonah, considering. 'No. It's honestly that in my experience it has no effect. Some are rewarded and others punished for the same act. That's the way of the world. But to receive no response at all, as if, hour by hour, I don't exist? I'm as effective as a ghost.'

'A well-placed ghost can nudge a needle. I'd gladly recruit an invisible man.'

'You intend to recruit me.'

'Would you be a bottle afloat with no message? Or seek to interfere for good in human matters? We've really got a good thing going, Jonah. An oblique nuisance that turns out to be real.'

'Fire and justice. Not very original.'

'The justice part is – it's that rare. Have you ever seen it done? You won't soon forget it!'

'That's true.'

'I don't hold with the notion,' Dollivar declared, 'that those who never feel a moment's pleasure cannot really know their own suffering. Mostly they still have eyes to see others' condition. But more than that, there is buried in us all that faint inchoate sense of hope, against which constant reality strikes off a recognisable flavour. Do you know some of our towers have chimneys extending their entire height, and children sweep every inch? Eaglet was once one of those wretches. It's not by chance that his appendages resemble sticks. Remember Dante's first word upon seeing the spires of hell: "Housing?" But as a consequence Eaglet can scale any height over any surface. Pound for pound he's stronger than a goat and is the most unpleasant and helpful lad I've ever laid eyes on.'

'This particular empire,' Sophie said, 'exhibits all the symptoms of decline – fear, confidence, volume. A late empire in all its detail of violence and foible.'

'It's the scum rises to the top, sport,' Dollivar said. 'The sort of evil you can recognise by the back of its head. You know what I mean. When you run with the ants, expect to be stepped on. Society's terms are exorbitant. The state holds our children ransom every day, hurts us by our virtues and disingenuously takes our exhaustion for assent. We are leveraged to the bone. This is why they can be so decisive, those moments when the demands of authority are most at odds with those of our own wellbeing. An honest day's work presupposes an honest day. They'll get you for giving the right answer out the wrong side of your mouth. And status is great for integration. It's total – the victim will actually defend it, work to uphold it. Loyalty to their particular jail cell. Explaining these facts is like trying to free a bird trapped in your room – you'll get attacked for your trouble.'

'I think it's a masochistic experience,' Sophie said. 'Constrained and grateful. Denied and excited.'

'Either way,' Dollivar concluded, 'if these shadows remain unaltered by the future, money will play the largest part in determining the course of history.'

'Why tell me all this?'

'Because I need you alive. Not on some one-way trip.' He exchanged a glance with Sophie. 'Let's take extremity for granted – together.'

'And then?'

'Rejoice with us by a broken window.'

Sophie rose and led Jonah slowly toward the door. 'Before rising to a challenge I determine the motive someone has for challenging me, and in what direction I would actually be moving. It's the work of a minute at most, and can spare years of wasted energy. And when people are surprised at my answering "No", it confirms I have made the right decision. Think about it Jonah. I'll contact you.'

'Yes, off you go,' Dollivar called. 'We can't have you having some raging catharsis in here while I'm trying to speak.'

Used to a chain of dismays, Jonah left the shack bejewelled out of his mind.

§

When Jonah was gone, Sophie sat flicking through *Darkle the Wise*. Dollivar had set a square mirror on the table and was carefully gluing a set of false muttonchops to his face. Except for the creaking, it was quiet for a while in the shack.

'Skinny isn't he?' said Tom at last.

'He's quite surprising,' said Sophie. 'The product of well-meaning but unimaginative parents. A brain like a solar event and a decency so mild it goes unnoticed. All that honesty with nowhere to go? No wonder he got educated to a standstill.'

'Quite,' said Dollivar, dabbing at his sideburns. 'You think that bookmite and his diagonal grievances can be any more than bones and a halo? Average man, need for approval would explain his dismal use of himself. Or a rather clenched reaction against that approval. And before he knows it his life's over. But your fellow's in an informed funk. Stymied by knowing the result of every action.'

'Everything tried so far. And he wants large effects, Tom. Besides, meekness serves as a fine preservative for rage. It can postpone its expression for decades.'

'Preservative?' Tom scoffed. 'Even his hackles are in a larval state.'

'His hackles are utterly exhausted. But despair sees in the dark and can't be surprised.'

'True, a sort of numb vigilance. But a life polished by ashes doesn't have much juice.'

'His brain is delicious. Just needs pepper. And he's at one of those crossroads in life where there's nothing in any direction. Believe me, someone so religiously precise has a release right under his head.'

'Well he's very taken with you. Thinks you're a pretty thing.'

'Yes, and if I'm this pretty at only twenty-two, think how I'll be at ninety. Did I hear you call yourself a hero?'

'Well I have the shabby charisma of a fugitive. Did I hear you encourage the lad to have nothing to do with us?'

'To think and feel deeply about his decision. Matters are lost when forced, Tom. An opened man is not the same as an open one. To correct things once and for all – that's what you want. You're a child, really. One of the signs that a moving body is intelligently controlled is that it changes direction. The soul should have flexible armour like a fish, thinner than skin and ready to shed. You're so stiff they'll be cutting your coat off.'

Tom pretended outrage, his moustache half hanging off. 'Anarchy, darling!'

'I think your love of disruption comes from the belief that you can command it, be at the crown of it. Do you expect people to stay the way you helped them to be? When they stop evading those things you keep pointing out, do you think you'll be popular? Celebrated? Will they be grateful? What are the chances, I wonder? A freed throng can be disappointing when it comes to it.'

'Oh I'll be swept away too, I know that. It'll be necessary. Scrubbed like a darts score and that's as it should be.' He pulled a shaggy wig from a carpetbag.

'You love the image,' Sophie prodded. 'And those stupid calling cards?'

'I know, those were stupid. I've given them up.'

'You're not Spartacus, darling. Or Petofi.'

'No, I'm the Rook. Well, we both are.'

'Jonah's been helping with this,' Sophie said, flipping the book. 'In the midst of a vacuum, how can a thing become so effervescent?'

'You've been hoping sideways again.'

'Yes. And blaming in my sleep.'

'I can't talk to you when you're like this.' He was forcing the wig this way and that on his head as he peered into the mirror. 'Can I be a rogue without further interruption? I need to discover what property Brewster's been buying. That magsman and his impossible power source. I don't have time for your enchanted errata.'

'This is something actually impossible,' Sophie urged, spreading the pages in his mirror so that he had to see it. 'A book that insists on itself and then changes its mind.'

Tom began to frown at the book in the mirror. Noticing his lack of protest, Sophie saw that the mirrored pages were a jumble of whirling, cascading words, threading into blurs and diving off in all directions.

6

A Hectic Commotion

The Elephant and Rascal was a pickled palace at the base of Ludgate Tower and here Lieutenant Lukas found himself enthroned. Today as always a former boxing bear called Paddy Sanders was staked to a sturdy pole in the beer garden, surrounded by festoons of thrown apples. It sat on its arse like a fat man, paws limp on its knees, and stared at Lukas with glue dripping from its eyes.

Lukas had drunk just enough to start seeing the back of his own head. He had been right about everything. He saw no need to represent the world in symbols when it was there and evident before him. Taking orders was nature's industry standard, tested by time and leaving plenty of leeway for his brand of amusement. People who claimed to have original ideas were surely making it up as they went along. Then he remembered General Varney's exhortation before the Pollifonty push –

'You lucky lads! You don't want to live forever!' –
and his mind stopped moving.

He became aware that a formidable-looking lady
had joined him under the awning. Her costume was
black as a dead coin and her crystalline hair had
been carved in imitation of a top hat. 'Drinking
alone?' she asked.

Her arrival was so well suited to his mental sprawl
he was easy with it. 'Me and the bear.'

She sat next to him on the bench. She smelt like a
piano. 'Is your name Lieutenant Francis Lukas?'

'Yes.'

'Will other people think so?'

'They will.'

'I'm Detective Inspector Nightjar, and there's
worse to come. Does the army dress in the dark
these days?'

'I'm off duty.'

'But it doesn't look good.'

'Have you seen Seventh Square? Scaffolding round
a lion. That doesn't look good.'

'Where is your beaver hat?'

'I lost it,' he said, though in fact he had sold it.
His debtors were keeping tabs on his billet and he
was heading for a bed under Ardwick Bridge. The
lure of tabulated chance. He would never wager on
slugs again.

'And your rifle?' she asked.

'Your hair. It's been carved to look like a topper.'

'One thing common to us all is that our hair is not important. Are you the beau of Sophie Shafto, of Shafto Steam and Boilers?'

'Forever getting to the point, that one. Where would we be if everyone got to the point?'

'You answer your own question. The better one is: when did you last see her?'

'Oh, yesterday. Superb and that's the trouble. A fury she is. Finer than flour I'd say, or ash. Smiles according to some mysterious schedule. Cute as otters in a basket. Felt sorry for me I think. For three weeks I was trapped in her good graces – she ended our dalliance, such as it was, and now I celebrate my freedom or something. Said I was a paper doll. Worse than a cad – a fool. A boring fool!'

'It's easy to be disappointed in a person when you've seen the blueprints for what they could have been. That's why angelic visitations are such a mixed blessing. Tell me a story, it needn't be ironclad. Did you quarrel?'

'Beautifully. I hope I know better than to agree with Miss Shafto – I'd miss the best of her. She's an amazing woman, and blinding when the fire's up. She'll enlighten you where you stand. I could spar with her till the cows lie down. But that wasn't even the reason she asked to meet. She had a book with her, *Darkle the Wise*, and wanted to know where I got it.'

'It was a gift? Apparently you know her well enough to give her a real book and not a looking-glass.'

'Girl's book-addled. Choosing ideas like bangles from a dress-up box. I found it in a cellar, under Robeck's mirror shop in Drood Street, a week ago. Place is run by a brittle bug sort of a man, feeble as a twig. Well I told her where I got the thing, she called me a parakeet, I think, and rode off.'

'What transport?'

'Half-carriage with a kettle pipe. Street cab. To go to that cellar I assume. Or else to the pile of haunted pork she's got for a father. They're thick as thieves. They bought a chessboard once and agreed to eat half each. He lives in a tin fort with figurines on the lawn. Never seen real action. The one time I met him he said I was a cricketball with eyes and arms. Because he has the money. A fortune? In steam? I'll be a skeleton with scanty skin and no faculties before I understand this bloody world.'

'Yes, strange that bones are the portion that prevails. Doesn't leave a very good impression.

What were you doing in the book cellar in the first place?'

'Eh?' Lukas noticed for the first time that the woman was writing things down in a notebook. He stared blearily at the bear for a while. Rain had started falling, darkening the animal's pelt. The rain was old, making everything look like newsprint. Maybe there'd be summer snow. 'Ah. Something I'd promised myself. A friend of mine, Nolan, recommended a fellow called Francois Villon. He used to sing Villon's stuff as everything exploded up around us. During an otherwise unremarkable frenzy he hollered out:

I hear a bird prattle
"You have all you need."
I hear its brain rattle
The size of a seed.

War's not all arrogance and peril you see. A great deal of it's quite dreary. Last time I saw Nolan his head was hanging off his shoulders like a mitten on a string. Death's not so romantic is it Inspector? Death shits in the sink and gives you a stare. It's been the ruin of many-a young man's posture. So I finally went to find some of that Villon, and as for the other book, the truth is Sophie mentioned it once, so when I saw it there I got it for her. In fairness the little bug man was damn near giving his stuff away. He said *Darkle* was "darkly funny". What does "darkly funny" mean?'

'It means "not funny". Do you object to the war, Mr Lukas?'

'Got me some scars, none of which I can make use of. The ladies who like it are an odd shower. Not for me to say.'

'Some men fight because they can't dance. Cavendish said that peace is a germ during that floating interlude between patients, and many people agree with her.'

'Germ or German?' Frank laughed. 'Me and Nolan, we'll meet again I'm sure of it. We'll be lined up chiming in the promised land like doll heads. Come to think of it I don't see how Sophie believes I can be dangerous and ineffectual at once. Bravery and compliance. A paradox, what it is. You'd have to fool yourself to act on it.'

'Well you still follow orders, I take it? If you've no notions of your own, pray to be of service. Do something to earn the ground's gravity at least. Do you have any ideas? Of your own, I mean.'

'I've started one or two. One or two. Mend my beer will you?'

The Inspector slid a full tankard aside to him. 'This is yours, Lieutenant. Villon called alcohol

"Infinity in a one-foot bottle" didn't he?'

'And there's the other song:

Learning love as an art,
I have lately been solaced.
There's a trick to a heart,
like the hinge of a mollusc.

Strange thing really, a writer. He tells lies in detail like a banknote. All that unasked-for paperwork is a sort of bureaucracy surely? A world that needs so many inspirational slogans to get through is probably defective.'

'I think it depends how you read it, Mr Lukas. Certain philosophers say the universe is a sentence that doesn't end, gobbling through clauses. Look at the city here, about us. The timber frame of each tower signifies a letter in an alphabet you possibly never learned. A quick scan of the skyline produces a paragraph that'll make your hair stand on end.'

'No, I don't see it that way at all. This city of yours is just a skirting board for the sky. And god is a bullet embedded in the ceiling. If I had money I'd be drinking in there with the gold-wrapped toffs.' He flicked a hand at King's Tower, atop of which the Skydome Tea Court allowed wealthy diners to observe airships arriving and departing from the nearby Fawcett mooring mast.

'Does that strike you as unfair? A life expressing

others' impulses while in uniform? Your brain, firing like a headless chicken, placing itself at others' command?'

'You're trying to goad me, madam, is that it? Any more pithy sayings before I go headlong into death and silence? I can't be goaded. Pride fills me up to the shoulders. And what's it all about anyway?'

'Sophie Shafto was abducted yesterday. The culprit is opposed to the foreign campaign. As any soldier with a clear head might be.'

'Ah.' Frank looked into the bear's many eyes. 'I've dug my own grave, I suppose. "To remain forever incomplete, like the bridges of Cambridge", that's what Sophie said. Sophie, abducted you say?'

'You have cut cards with the devil, Lieutenant.' The Inspector closed her notebook. 'I don't blame you for not wanting to look down.'

'Oh I'll drink till I'm level with the smalls of the ground. We have to go all the way in a world like this. Malignant dogma? I can't get enough of it!'

'Perhaps the crime that dooms your life is only one step on from your current excitement. Many a drunken man has hunted the sandwich he had in his hand.' Inspector Nightjar stood.

'You expect me to have your mischief for you, Detective? Go have your own, eh?'

'I think I may say without fear of contradiction,

you are an ape sir, and not a good one.'

'And what constitutes a good ape?' Frank scoffed.

'Self-respect,' the Inspector stated, and walked into the darkness of the bar.

Frank lunged after her, halting on the beer-embalmed floor. He could make nothing out. Blackness blotted and bloomed in his eyes. He had the strange sensation that he was woefully unprepared for what he himself was about to shout. 'My heart is a shoe full of blood, what do you think of that?'

§

Nightjar's notes: When a fool speaks his mind, hold onto your hat. Lieutenant Francis Lukas served a year in the Transvaast under Lord Ruthven and General Varney and is currently on leave. Hardly the dashing cad I expected, his disjointed outlook makes him eminently available to any authority. His worldview is a hectic commotion which he expresses with the compensatory precision of a drunkard. Costume has a complicated frontis like gilded ribs. A playing card but more predictable. Hooligans shouldn't be boring but they are. Money troubles? Borrowed pride is thin stuff. Perhaps he considers turning boltroon. At least subterfuge has structure. These actions of his are sludge. A plodding accomplice? Talking to him's like shaving a wooden leg. The inside of the alehouse was smoked like a haddock. Reminder to free bear.

7

An Advanced Pawn

Jonah collapsed home dizzy with rain. From Lasher's Wharf he had negotiated a chaos of platforms, galleys and cables in a tribal, torrential state of mind, a torn-apart sensation with flashing edges. Sophie had stunned him into a bedazzling relish, glutinous and avid. Within seconds she had filled every corner of his life. He was conscious of the entire surface of his body. Every nerve about him crackled with a kind of glee, an ecstatic strain which distracted him from the fact that a fall from here would bring his legs to a shattering end. Rain was fizzing around chimneys and ledges. What appeared the high refinement of the average gargoyle was surprisingly grimy up close, but they all had a smile for him. He finally reached the sweet miracle of solid ground near Garkley stables. His jacket had torn on some wire and his shirt was grimy with rust. He strode toward Drood Street. The rain had let up after putting a gloss on the coloured towers and they looked like a thousand dipped candles. The sky was a clean million-year-old blue. He waved hello to several strangers. Exhilarating jeopardy. Sophie writing fire with her bare hands. Thomas Dollivar and his terrifying morale. He could still hear the twanging of guywires and high-tension dissembly.

He let himself into Robeck's Reflectives. Standing mirrored a hundred times in the centre of the shop was what appeared to be a monstrous crow. 'A book is like you and me,' it said.

§

Nightjar did not introduce herself to the sickly youth who entered in a torn clawhammer coat. He was leaking rain and bespattered with mud and straw. In response to the passphrase he looked like he'd been walloped with a club. She supposed that finding her standing there like a thunderstorm was a surprise, but it was curious that he evinced guilt when it was she who had trespassed.

Emerging from his stupor, he approached a tall wall mirror and pushed its edge – the whole thing inverted counterclockwise, the strange lack of movement in its content making it seem that only the frame had revolved. Then he pushed inward and the wall opened. She followed him down a metal stairwell into an all-surrounding silo where books glowed like the dainties in a patisserie.

This place had everything. At a glance she spotted at least a dozen books she had thought vapourized by neglect. There was *Absalom's Fall, Fugue's Almanac, The Seven Heads of Fred Bayle, Pilot and the Gravefish, Lives of the Alien Saints, The Slurping Hostage, Last Year in the Skull, The Blame Index of Edgar Finch* and *Ken's Vortex*. Richly brocaded spines of purple and gold. A red book suspended in a jar of vinegar. A book with handles like a valise. A book like a heart, a book like a bug belly, a book like a turnip, a book like a bellows, a book so big and armoured it must be opened by the tip of a sword. Books of bird reluctance and other fugitive genres. There was even a section for invertebrates, unspined sheafs and bundles.

And not a mirror in sight. The looking-glass book had begun as a fad among the harmless classes, consisting of a handsome leather binding in which several mirrors could be flipped like pages, thus presenting one's own face at every turn. It wittily combined philosophical symbolism with purest vanity. Now they were everywhere and few people read the real thing. A place like this was a storehouse of renegade thought and rich misadventure. Nightjar removed her gloves.

'Can I interest you in *Travels of Enrico the Lizard*?' said the morpish boy, and began clattering back and forth between the stacks like a wind-up figure. 'Or *The Secret Curve of Finias Runk*? Perhaps I can tempt you with, yes, here it is – *Doctrine and Ritual of the Master Chef*, a mad book in which everyone is elaborately angry. *The Conkhurst Plea*, a book which begins in monotone and ends in colour, with basenotes of resentment. And this – a barbed book. See the talons holding it together? Ah! How about arts and crafts - *Here's To Porcelain*. Or if that's not in your wheelhouse, *Bonvolio's Treatise On The New Nature*. A doctrine so labyrinthine is obviously hiding something – see if you can spot it! Biographies from rattle to death rattle! Cram's inscrutable life, *Me and the Monkey and Ten Others*, really a list of excuses. Allegra Presto's three-part memoir, *The Endless Unlocking*, *My Mounting Impatience*, and *A Stunned Exasperation*.' He scooted up a ladder and returned with a plump edition of *Madoc's Mechanical Mythologies*, and something else. 'This is a *Book of False Hours*. Can you feel the vibrations of waste it exists in?' It was freezing to the touch. He fetched her *The Book of Second Thoughts*, its sickly pages smelling of violets. '*The Mutiny Gospels*, a kaleidoscopic lion's throat, freaky cheap. *The Avocado Ticket*. A

taxonomy of misgivings. *Pumperson's Heartbreak*.
You've never felt despair like this, I promise you.
My Friend the Crab. That one's a puzzle. *Quite's
Book*. Victor Quite theorized that there may be
integers between the alphabetic characters we know.
You've heard that there is "a world of difference"
between one thing and another. These worlds,
secreted everywhere, are my fascination!'

'More than one of them may turn out to be a
world of trouble.'

He seemed not to have heard her, and was dashing
around so quickly it was drying him out. 'Fiction!
*The Redundant Rescue, Scott Stander and the Stigma
Lady, The Groggy Intruder, John Coriander the
Turquoise Engineer*. Ah, here's *Mr Fondwolf Stole My
Lips* – a scream tolerably expressed but losing a lot in
translation from the Spanish. *The Chronicles of Grave
the Pirate*. Sarcasm on the high seas. And illustrated.
Here we see the supercilious hero smirking into a
headwind. And I recommend *The Sky Doesn't Know
It's Thursday* by Penny Artesia, because I can't
help myself, it's a pity isn't it? *Gulliver Ink and
the Undermine*, a story in which everyone wakes
up to find everything's on the slant. A book in
praise of sleep, *Goodnight Saves the World*. And
another Bardo book in which people's ears start
proliferating far beyond utility. *More Inconvenience*,

an odd story about a tall building with each floor existing in a different year. *The Stump*, in which a parliament of bandaged statues stands propped and tilted in utter silence for eight years. And we have to read all about it. *The Failure's Apprentice*. The world ends, the whole family is sorry. *Songs of Experience*. Blake bet on a horse no-one else could see didn't he? Darwin. It's one puffin after another with him. Newton. He took a tough stand on immensities. *The Paloma Cypher*, a secret history disguised as a stamp album. *Harrow's Arcana*, a prayer book designed to contain a pistol. I also have a first edition of the *Wolf Dollar Catalogue*, plus *Stain's Flood Almanac*, *The Invisible College End of Term Report* and the only authenticated journal of Jesus's polar expedition. And if those are not to your taste, this book is a Faraday cage which allows no ideas to enter or emerge. It did very well, as you can imagine.'

Nightjar had a look at it. *Prevarication By Gaslight*. He brought her more curios – a book of reversed curses, a book of flavoured pages, a book containing real plants and butterflies pressed flat out of sudden fright – but what interested her was a little round table at the centre of the subterranean reading parlour. It was cluttered with coins and sugarcubes, a pyramid kettle, a bottle of Morrigan's Nerve

Tonic, spectacles with blackcherry lenses and a papier mache roc egg. There were throw beads, diablo dice and a deck of banjax tarot. It seemed the bookherd had exhausted all means of making a decision. A copy of *The Hammertail* lay amid the arcana, a smaller book poking from it as a bookmark. *Truth's Flying* something.

'This may interest you, ma'am,' the bookherd hailed her. 'Benn Hellebore's *Varieties of Received Experience*, a study of social hysterias, from faith in the police to the Glass Delusion.'

'Glass Delusion?'

'Of the sixteenth century. A mass hysteria for believing one's body is made of glass. It was particularly prevalent among the ruling classes, who believed it was an inherited blood sickness, and that the only end to it was to exhume and destroy their ancestors. The story goes that these exhumed bodies were found to be completely transformed into glass, and that smashing them with a wooden hammer lifted the affliction.'

'You are a mine of information, Mr Robeck.'

'Oh I can find anything in here. It's as familiar to me as the roof of my own mouth. A book may be saddled like a warty toad, but smuggle it in wineskins? That's added value. The truth's a lot more spicy when provided by privateers. It's said that witches have made a safe store of every seed, against the end of days. You know the old seer. A book lays apparently dead for centuries and then in a single day it sends fresh green shoots all over the place.'

'I've listened with interest to your sales pitch, Mr Robeck,' Nightjar told him good-humouredly. 'But what if the seed you mention contains colours unseen for centuries? Or worse still, introduces a chemical which in combination with the present day sparks colours never seen before? What you describe might be called a preserved germ and a plague, or some other calamity. Certain ideas fire a fellow up. Oh, heaven knows I don't mean to frighten you but I should introduce myself. Detective Inspector Nightjar. A little bird with a brain coincidentally the size of a seed told me you saw young Sophie Shafto yesterday, heiress to the Steam and Boilers fortune. We think she may have got into difficulties or run into the wrong crowd. She was here after a book. I should mention that dishonesty or "Welsh conjecture" is recorded and may be used against you.' She flipped open her notebook.

Jonah had stiffened in place. 'Yes,' he said blandly, looking at nothing in particular. 'Yes, *Darkle the Wise*, about some capering sorcerer in a spangle hat. I happen to know where the author lives. I told her where to find him in Bombley, and sent her on her way. I'll do the same for you. I've nothing interesting to hide especially.'

'Where is she now?'

'Will you believe me if I tell you I don't know. You could ask her swain, the soldier. He got it for her, I remember, several days ago, and a little book of poems. The *Salt Bible* I think it was, by Villon.'

'Villon! When alive he was no more than "a spark through a turtle-star". They made the legends later, didn't they? It's easy to be fierce in amber. No follow-through. We may sit in a corner and think we've changed the world! I imagine patrons confide in you as in a priest?'

'Oh I don't know about that. I'm not much for confidences. I hold a shell to my ear and all I hear are accusations.'

The lad was very twitchy. One moment he performed a meaningless smile and the next he was puffing out his cheeks like a blowfish. His shirt was stained brown. Sophie Shafto seemed to have an odd effect upon people.

'Accusations? Is that so? How do you feel about our aggressions abroad?'

'I'm sure at the outset it seemed like a good idea.'

'Ale is golden till it comes up again, is that it? I see you're reading *The Hammertail*. It's not lean.'

'A dalmatian is lean. And unnatural. That book's big enough to embed your face in – why there's a whole world in there, annotated in a frenzy! Apparently a whale has ten hearts, all in a row like bloomers on a washline!'

'What's this tucked inside, philosophy? A notion that has been dead fifty years expels a gas some find enticing.'

'This might interest someone with your kind of mind, Inspector,' said Robeck, moving nimbly to a contraption balanced on a pile of newspapers. 'A Hidden Sholes typewriter. The swirled surface design incorporates a Taoist yin and yang swirl into the type well.'

Nightjar went over and regarded it diffidently. 'It looks like an Oriental church organ.'

'Amerikaan actually. Beginners' luck at genocide but more inventors per square inch, chewing tobacco and so forth. Clark Dyer was in the air and laughing before the Brunel Committee smuggled him over here. He wasn't just sitting there running an onion ranch.'

'Are you nervous, Mr Robeck?' She drew a sheet of paper from the machine and inspected the few lines of type. 'You wrote this, I take it? "The forest, a chamber of small beasts. Till I got there." This is your opening line? "Unpick my skull and remind me I'm a toy". "Dark daisies". "Scene two. A lighthouse full of wet thorns." "The punctual burden of awaking".'

'Well I *am* punctual, what of it?' Jonah snapped, snatching the paper from Nightjar's hand and talking a mile a minute. 'I have a theory, Inspector, or fancy perhaps, about an enchantment which stops people from writing anything interesting, much in the way that those with money lose all will to do anything inventive with it. Beat me to a jelly if you like, but we do them a mis-service to believe this dross is what they meant to write! No-one is so dull, so witless! Surely imagination is capable of more than a king or queen!' He gave an odd shriek of hilarity which seemed to emanate from his shoulder.

'This is hardly a cool appraisal of the circumstances,' stated Nightjar patiently, the hand in her pocket clasping her service pistol. 'What you're describing is literary determinism, and I believe it serves a purpose. What if all the ideas fended off by humanity found a way in? For the fellow with the entry hole, it would be rather intense. You seem agitated, young man. I'm aware that I've startled you. Let us sit down at this little table and discuss our concerns in a convivial manner. No need for alarm. I've no wish to "beat you to a jelly" as you suggest. When you pay for a meal, is it a counterblow? A reckoning needn't be confrontational.'

They sat at the table. Nightjar kept a kindly look on her face, but Robeck was not at ease. He looked as if he expected the room to tilt and sink like a ship at any moment.

'That shibboleth at the door,' the Inspector said. 'I know it's traditional for these places, but do you believe it? That everyone is doing their best? There's a myth that villains don't know they're the villain. Well, knowing humanity, what do you think?'

'Specific cases can support anything,' the young man stated cautiously. 'A lot of unnecessary complication comes of the belief that people are only pretending to be stupid.'

'Perhaps,' said Nightjar vaguely, frowning at him. 'You know, in my profession, I must walk a fine line, Mr Robeck – times being what they are. To think without being precocious, to speculate without creativity, to leap without conspicuous genius. It has to happen afterneath and underwards, as it were. Most of the time it's just a feeling. At other times it's filled with complex data. Informational architecture. My colleagues at Caledonia Tower think evil's just the detailed side of a spider. Their impatience pushes the cork into truth, tainting it. I do it differently, allowing time to reveal all the parallels and patterns of chance. A confluence of errors may operate as exactly as any mechanism. Now, if I'm right –' She tipped the placeholder out of *The Hammertail* and lifted the heavy volume, peering at its broad mottled flank. She slanted the big book's spine, its pages separating like gills to reveal a colourful picture along its fore-edge. It depicted Captain Abed riding the whale over a rainbow. 'All this information, Mr Robeck, and all I have to do is look at it side-on and bend it a little to get a different picture. Like an oblique split through stacked dimensions. There are still a few facts left, for those who care. Isn't that why you gathered this rather impressive library?' She dropped *The Hammertail* back on the table.

'Is it a crime, yet, to quote Violaine?'

'When a thing becomes clandestine of its own accord, the law becomes envious. Choose your secrets well, Mr Robeck. If you keep a thing chained in your basement you will find yourself beholden to it. Heresy, for instance, is defined against an alternate belief. Not a very precise method. Treason goes the same way. Some would say that this intercommunication you have here, when honest, this interchange of ideas, will be the end of civilisation – yes, even that. Not exploded but revealed and clarified, in all its colour and variation. Is humanity equipped, Mr Robeck? Equipped to know everything? Is this not the purview of god itself?'

'Well it's nothing to the torments enacted in the poulterers opposite, I promise you. But I daresay some things are beyond us. To truly perceive eternity you'd at the very least have to think about it forever.'

'That brings us to the heart of the matter. Imagine the nightmare of being unable to fully forget anything, to hold the injustices and contradictions of ages in a single design. No selection or denial. The disappointment at seeing clearly how little has been achieved by our best minds and hearts. That's how to go mad, or stark sane. My advice to a young man – may I give it? – is to stop pestering yourself. Stop yearning for the excesses of the Vivid Age and the antics of the Troy Fool and his cornucopian head. That was, what, twenty years ago.'

'Might as well be a century,' Jonah said.

'It is remarkable how fast certain fads are swept off, as if under embarrassment. Or orders. When a culture changes, things are thrown away wholesale, as after a fire or the death of a relative. Troy Fool! It sounds like a trifle!' She pushed her notebook

over at him. 'Write the author's address in there.'
She snapped up the little philosophy book from the
table. 'And I'm confiscating this. It'll be one less
thing for you to worry about. That pulpy gubbins
in your head is eating you alive.'

He scribbled in the notebook and returned it to
her, his stark face white as lightning.

§

*Nightjar's notes: Jonah Robeck. Big eyes and a face like
an open window. Wears a grubby tube-coat with a
tail like a tuning fork. What he said wasn't what I
wanted, but it didn't lack interest. I expected someone
with his mind in a cosy impasse, cornered by displaced
detail into what the Orientals call the Hell of Measures.
But behind the scavenance of a paraphernalian he
is a man of the book. Such men are particular, if
they are to be found at all today. He would have you
think he procures rare books intended for a limited,
reasonable audience, a quaint misconduct. In fact he
is a strong filter-feeder trafficking in medical-grade
exhilarants and has done it long enough that he's clogged
with glittering astronomies. Tense as a diamond and
pointing off in as many directions. One moment
exhibiting a wild disagreement and another seized
by a sort of pressurised laughter which goes off at an
angle. Only a bungled abyss can generate that kind*

of merriment. A sickly soul rattled into defiance? A breakdown for a cause? Or he simply has an abundance of nervous energy but no application – and so, settling for that which requires least effort, he cannot stop talking? What he said was very like the truth – I spotted the resemblance at once. But few people radiate a diabolical criminality. A dog sits happily amid its crimes. A cat has everyone blaming each other.

8

Done With Mirrors

Sophie rapped her rolled umbrella on the door of Robeck's Reflectives. Jonah had closed up, but now emerged from the gloom and unbolted. There was summer daylight to burn. He looked surprised at her dunnage. She was wearing glasses and a white origami gown with more secret compartments than a writing desk, plus a cream topper with three more pairs of spectacles stacked on the fascia. 'I need your help,' she told him. 'Who knows the most about mirror-making?'

'Evelyn Brae at Ludi's in Eighth Square. She's my aunt. She can see the silver bloodstream of a mirror. The pink umbrella doesn't match.'

'It was very expensive. I'm playing the part of a journalist called Kelly Mayshark. Come and introduce me.'

'Is this what a journalist dresses like?'

'I have no idea really. Why do you look so worried,

have you eaten an eel?'

'I was visited today by an officer of the state police.' He shrugged on his coat.

'I see! Did they give a name?'

'Inspector Nightjar. Exacting and un-predictable, a confusing combination.'

'How thrilling! She's a legend! Incongruously competent and honest! Her life is pure hell!'

'Well, talking to her was like being closed very gradually into an iron maiden.'

'Fabulous!'

'She made off with your berserk manifesto.'

'Ah. I see.'

He locked the shop behind him, following her across the street to a Jackney cab. 'She doesn't know what she's got but she'll realise soon. I sent her to Carpstein.'

'Listen,' she said as they got inside the cab. The boy Eaglet was sat in a corner, silently reading a penny dreadful titled *Pike and the Eyes*. He was done up in black and had swipes of soot on his face. 'After seeing the mirrorsmith we'll go back to the shop to regroup and change costumes. I'll hire the coach for the rest of the night but not the coachman. I need you to drive.'

'Drive? I don't know horses, Sophie. They're gigantic.'

'Can you operate a Sparks Landau?'

'No.'

'Then it's the coach, isn't it? Eaglet and I have a job in Lasker Street. You're our escape driver. It'll solemnize our understanding.'

'Why, is Tom busy?'

'Yes. Building a bomb small enough for a hatbox.'

'Really?'

'Of course not, you fantastic mooncalf, he's doing research in places where I'll be recognised.'

'Mooncalf, why?'

'You have possibly the best brain I've met, Jonah. It makes me ache really, a sort of a glottal ache in the middle of the air, except for the regrettable fact that you use it almost entirely against yourself. That, my dear, is damned unattractive.'

'My brain.'

'Yes. I had a bloody dream about it last night. It was dripping honey all over me. The sort of dream that comes of sleeping on a high gantry. As beds go a reinforced bulkhead is rather unforgiving.'

'You're in a good mood.'

Sophie was in a good mood. She thought about Nightjar. A mind worth its salt was a perfectly precise turmoil. The coach was passing through Redchapel toward Tower Hill. She saw street preachers, feral jesters and children playing nought-

and-stick. Wire-scryers who told the future from machine guts. A tramp lay grinning like a bog body. Another stood chewing at a violin. A magician disported himself as a herring, fooling no-one. People living next to nothing.

Shifting her attention, Sophie noticed Jonah staring at her. 'Maybe you think I'm a romantic,' she said, 'posing as revolutionary and spending a fortune on an armoured brolly. The Shaftos are of northern stock, Jonah, and my father's title a return on an investment. But it's true when you're born red-handed as I was, I could have been undone by entitlement. Amazing the wasted time which is forgiven if it's spent in company. Modulating one's screams to conform with polite dinner conversation. I adore a breach of etiquette – I see scrambling treasure in the gap.'

'I formed no great opinion of you until that thing with the book.'

'You should see what I'm writing now. It's getting smaller and more flavourful, like cooking meat. Anyone who speaks with their own voice gets noticed or ignored – which is worse I wonder?'

Sophie remembered her disastrous efforts to adapt. She had been born into a dazzling tedium made up of copied particles in suspension. She found the same sentiments on show everywhere like the time on every clockface. Her propensity for calm had provoked immediate suspicion. In fact she was regarded with such a united front of bemusement she could not entirely dismiss the notion that it was planned. To be misunderstood at such breakneck speed surely required a run-up. Thank heavens for the liquid gold of solitude and the accident that thought was inherently clandestine! Today she understood the pressure upon everyone to tell the truth only when the tide was right and to walk through life with heart averted. To her this society was a collection of hardshell dolls clattering together, every one containing an unacknowledged human being. Those who refused to own their humanity – and which she had once treated as the wooden dummies they purported to be – she now regarded with a mixture of patience, pity and occasional exasperation.

'Lockstep, Jonah – the ability to stop being an individual on a sixpence – is beyond me. Even a tree stops somewhere, but it doesn't start being something else. I know a collective torment may appear harmonious. We may even adjust our position to one from which it seems all the more so. When I was a child my father absolutely forbade me to say or do anything interesting. Imagine the kerfuffle the first time I burst out thinking in public!

He gave me such a complicated talking-to I lost the thread. For a while I spoke with my mouth closed so as not to spoil people's day, but the effect was quite odd. Very briefly I tried their way. Man-made law deemed me an object so I would act as such. Be ingenuous and miss the subtleties. I can't remember how I justified this position to myself. The prevailing outcry was all about automata, perhaps I used that. But I found it took reserves of energy I could better use on almost anything else. I was so very far into myself, I could not be persuaded otherwise. Finally I was driven to commit acts of such common sense, I would never be forgiven. Doing good here's a protest, it turns out.'

'How did you survive this long?'

Sophie remembered something she'd seen in a book of Sufi zingers, *Don't talk about every bird you see.* 'There's a strategy. Pretend to be slowed in the ooze of their evaluations and simply continue. Attend but don't take root. Don't fritter away your euphoria among strangers. And the writing is good therapy.'

'Well, I've abandoned my own efforts, though I hoped to leave something behind.'

'Woolly hair on a barbwire fence?'

'Oh it's tickling to adjust surfaces, but the essence of things never changes does it?'

'Is this why you stand silent as a chess man before the worst injustices?'

'The future surrounds our decisions. That's what stops me. Be honest, Sophie, we have no idea what we've lost or gained by all this industrial acceleration.'

'Oh, I have a rather good idea. Old empire, its stupid tongue flopping and slapping like a belt, while purporting to lead the future on a chain. "It'll get worse before it gets better" – the fact that this statement is perennial should tell you something. They'll suck the future out of you, Jonah, and give it their meaning. They'll wear you for a hat they've forgotten they're wearing.'

'Is the alternative this seven-door farce you've got for a lifestyle, with eight names and an overnight bag full of moustaches? You're Tom's mollisher aren't you?'

'Not in the physical sense – I haven't the tool for that. And as for who follows whom, we both put up. I suppose we agree but occupy different ends of the idea. His inflexibility is an inspiration when it doesn't annoy, and we'll certainly die, separately or together.'

'It sounds like revolution at the sweet spot of underdog yearning and kitsch iconography.'

'That's not the sweet spot, darling, believe me. I

don't carry a picture of Danton in a locket.'

'I suspect the romance of the barricades falls apart when you're shot in the eye.'

'Not if you expect it. Dying young doesn't always mean half-finished.'

'Now you're confusing me.'

'I don't mean to. This canned deathwish of yours strikes me as almost the least interesting course available to you. Your rebellion and your alternative to it – all copies. Have you considered suddenly bolting open like a metal claw?'

'Claw,' Jonah murmured wearily. 'No it never occurred to me...'

'I think real empathy is of the body, Jonah, like a blush. It's not enough to just be vigilant of the gearworks around you. It's true that the traction you provide is minimal, a speck amid the mechanism, but awareness of its architecture increases only slightly the chances of escape.'

'If a speck provides no traction, how does the mill work?'

'Millions of victims are substance enough. Steam, the new voltaics – they're better or worse tools, when the real question is, who wields them? It's demeaning, really, to have oppressors so dumb. But they use a tried-and-tested system. Tom says they're reckless to the health and life of the workers – but recklessness implies a judgement in approach. They don't regard the workers as human at all, and so there's no question of recklessness. We're born and go up in smoke – for what? Society's gears apparently. Not everyone would see it that way, given the chance. It remains to be seen whether these conundrums are as nourishing as bread, but I suspect not.'

'You realise the betterment of mankind may be a kind of personal over-compensation?'

'So is its opposite and much in between.'

'We're going in circles.'

'Yes we are. Tight little circles.'

Eaglet sighed heavily. He had heard it all before. Arriving at Ludi's Glassworks, they left the boy in the cab. 'I should warn you,' Jonah told Sophie as they walked into the warehouse – it had once been a trolley depot and the old tramlines still scored the floor. 'Mirror people are creepy. It seems they're honour-bound to be peculiar.'

'"Peculiar" just means precision with a different subject,' called a pointy crone with wraithy dunnage and diaphanous hair, emerging from behind a large chrome swan. She looked like a gnarled fairy.

'Hello Auntie,' said Jonah with a grin, his breath clouding. It was chilly in the warehouse but none of those present cared for the strictures which would have them disown their own nose steam, nor for the jerking head movements involved. 'This is my friend, er, Betty Sparhawk, a columnist who is interested in mirrorwork.'

'Is this how they dress, Joe? Hello missy. I can give you five minutes. Plus its reflection makes ten.'

'Thank you. I saw something strange in an ordinary mirror recently and need to know how it happened. I don't know anything about the trade.'

'I see. Well, the old wisdoms would have us believe this: just as, behind a mirror and its deep image, is an actual hidden depth, there is an unseen mechanism behind every moment. Half the content of a world is in its mirrors. You may have seen the operations of something true without obscurity. Stare into the depths of this reef mirror!' She gestured airily at a harp-shaped mirror which rested against some statuary. 'A delay glass, which will show the customer's image from years before – the younger the image the more expensive the mirror. What is your pleasure?'

'Don't look,' said Jonah tightly.

'If the other side is merely a mirror image,' said Sophie, 'it contains no truly new information.'

'Two opposites imply everything in between, to the functioning mind. Some say you can't see the world as it is within an unbroken mirror – only a shattered one can reflect it aright. I say, gaze into this beauty – an elevened mirror! It will present the scene with only one small detail out of place – and the anomaly will always be of significance!' She danced over to a tall triangular mirror and flourished her bony hands across it.

Jonah was tired and impatient. 'We are not here to buy, Auntie.'

'Don't have room to swing a cat? This mirror can be used for storage. Tuck your things aside and just out of view.' She indicated a mirror the size of a small cupboard.

'It's a mirror on the front of cupboard, Auntie, as you well know.'

'The fabric of a mirror is agreeable to certain manipulations. The adjustment which takes place through a mirror is survivable. It is not an addition nor a subtraction. And certainly it is no great matter to slip in something interesting. A mirror reverses right and left but not up and down – clearly its world is subject to the same gravity as ours.' Brae flailed her arms at a chunky mirror like an altarpiece. 'When someone dies we place a black veil over the mirrors to prevent god's clowns from making their mischief. And it has always been this way. Have you ever heard a storm on the other side of a mirror, reporter lady? Have you seen rain pelt the other side of the glass?'

'These folk stories are delightful,' Sophie smiled, 'but I don't grasp –'

'Then there is the architecture beyond the door in a mirror, very strange constructions to be sure. Those inverted acres can be bought for nothing. No trespass, no poaching. Behold the Lincoln glass!' She pranced over to a round mirror big enough to step into. 'What if I told you this world of ours was in fact made left-handed, but the right-handed are using it? This life is a system of agonies, but across there? Everything points the other way. All patterns are reversed. And who's to say that pain mightn't point away into relief? No wonder we are haunted by that reverse room behind us.'

'I can't use any of this,' Sophie said.

Brae waved at a bulging mirror of golden glass. There was black water trickling from its base, puddling. 'The feeding of mirrors is a matter of great particularity. Give them plenty of movement, lots of depth and some variation. To have one facing an often-used door is ideal, giving it glimpses of the hallway beyond. A mirror that's fed no movement at all will tend to lose its colour, or even empty completely like a milky eye.'

'This is artisanal nonsense, Auntie – and insulting to my friend.'

The mirrorsmith scowled. 'If your father could hear you he'd crawl out of a mirror and claw your face. And if he saw what you'd done to the shop, he'd drag you screaming into the mirror with him. Using Robeck's Reflectives as a front for a book cellar! I knew you when you were no taller than an Italian. You were always soft-hearted, lacking confidence and beholden to everyone. The first time your father caught you reading a book he should have smashed a mirror over your head. Books, Joe, are full of retorts to remarks long lost. Truth is pursued by its own tail. Counterclockwise round a bonfire.'

'Well now I'm a full-blown man, Auntie, and I daresay in the way. But I read to feed, not to get in a ghost's good graces. I don't think it's a dead thing. A meaning from a book may surprise us like a scorpion escaped from a paperweight.'

'If that's what you want a mirror's good for a scare, as when there's an unfamiliar doll reflected there. A doll with ill-informed views and real hair. Tee-hee!'

'What did I tell you,' Jonah whispered aside to Sophie.

'And if that weren't enough, Joe, your front's stuffed with glass books. The very thing that's cheapening the mirror trade and the book trade both! Put that in your article, reporter lady!'

'I have to stock a few, Auntie. The demand.'

'Is it so low then,' Sophie asked, 'for people to look to themselves rather than the notions of others?'

'If that was what they were doing it'd be a fine thing. But the low power of a looking-glass book is that it only shows them a face. Bibliomancers, their mission used to be, "What nonsense is it that spares us the truth?" Now, certain inferior mirror-makers, they've realised that the sight of one's own face, beautified, is all that any poor soul needs. A revelation of empty, urgent light. The genius of fabricating mirrors in the shape of a book, reflecting back only what a supposed "reader" already feels! The bare-faced lack of invention! The Surfacers' Guild used to be a wryly ironic title – now it seems fitting, eh?'

Sophie made a motion to leave. 'Thank you for being so helpful, Auntie.'

'It steals more than your face, missy! A glass book allows a person to look all day at their own surface, while appearing deep.'

'Many people's depths are a knotted horror they'd rather avoid,' Jonah argued.

'Honest humour dissolves those knots. Failing that, we must wait for time to rot 'em. In the meantime better to head out and bag a blue sky with your own eyes. I pray on my haunches that those little mirrors get hungry and start to bite them who are fawning over themselves. Bite! Believe me, you don't want to be eaten by a mirror. These fools with looking-glass books, they're tempting fate. Bite!'

'She means well,' Jonah told Sophie as they left the warehouse. 'She's an illusionist really, and it's rather more serious than that.'

9

A Test of Patience

Inspector Nightjar, too, was in a trance of disinterest.

'I was born in 1810 in Surrey,' said Hugo Carpstein, 'exactly the thing I'd been trying to avoid. All of a sudden real and miniscule, my first cell was eager enough to multiply. Well, organic life's looking for trouble, isn't it? But without it there'd be less of everything every day. They scrutinized a minute under a microscope once, and the blooming geometries of hell had them screaming. We have the right in old age to visit old faults and find them golden. In my case, a recitation of my errors would char your ears. Oh I had amusement where I could find it. Pulling floppy animals from the ocean. Planting radishes on contested land. Abruptly crouching during conversation. And now the *danse macabre* of owning a cat. When the solar system tied the knot, it didn't know what it was getting itself into did it? But life's like squirrel meat, you make do. Look at this great slab of a head. It's a fantastic one given the casual manner in which I came by it but I was lumbered with the ancillary agony of a strenuously pounding brain. Truth regularly snapped within an inch of my face, and I tell you Inspector, truth is a terrapin angel – all real and all wrong. And that's when the accident happened. The least I can do is open the scratched door of myself, I thought. Dip my pen in the dirty night sky. Pour treasure upon the unready! Every step was met with gusts of refusal. In fact I was so exactingly detained I became suspicious. It later emerged that there was an entire planet in the way. Apparently I'm only here to provide scale. Got the Anachron Award for best newcomer. That award was a baboon's welcome. But when I saw the error of my ways it was such a compelling shape I decided to continue. I got in some of the real stuff. I was telling mighty truths and people just bunched around me like bananas! Whenever I lost hope, which was most of the time, I judged others and found them sorely wanting. But should I assert anything in bones so temporary? There are a finite number of lessons to learn here. That the chrysalis of an empire is prettier than what emerges. That laws shall be enforced by those who least understand them. Don't yell condolences. You know the rest, Inspector. My words are muffled by my own massive face, as you can see, and these enormous beards I've been working on for forty years. The body, a life, it's like a book, a detailed potion poured into the void. So I find myself with a cat I can't impress no matter how hard I try and an umbrella like a mosquito's chin. My face is a cracked wall and I'm behind it still. My hair ceased to have any value long before it abandoned me. My most enduring book might achieve a few unraked ashes in an archive. There it is, I'm fat and there's nothing more to be done. I'm the elephant in my own room. My gums are in tatters. I wake every day into the flavour of a dying body. And to complicate things, I didn't get away with it. Time to hitch up my skin and leap into the afterlife. My shoes will no longer grit beneath me. In summary: I set off in disguise and am now naked and bouncing on my own balls, shrieking like a maniac.'

Carpstein was sat in a sort of poulticed armchair, his legs crossed like a Turk. On the floor nearby was a loaf-shaped cat of tremendous size, which he reached for like a drowning man. The room was littered with slaughtered books and bandaged furniture.

Nightjar was standing in the middle of the room

with her pen poised above her notebook. She took
a controlled breath and composed herself. 'Mr
Carpstein. I came here on a police-issue kettle car
known as a bonesplitter. I expect to be seeing my
own liver in a few hours. I have asked you for a
factual account of Sophie Shafto's visit to your
residence yesterday. In return you have listed a
dozen snags I can't imagine and charred, as you put
it, my ears with an inferno of self-pity.'

'You have it exactly, Inspector. As a butterfly
can't see its own wings we can't see our own evil.
Only others' wings. And you did the right thing
coming to me. I had a sort of fever-dream once that
my life was just the slow elongation of a molten
error. I've trudged a thousand miles for a conclusion
I knew in advance. Who says I'm a wise man? Can I
confide in you, Detective? This is the first time I've
had a bluebottle in my parlour. I suppose I've a few
old-fashioned transgressions, the small kind you can
put a cherry on. Morality's a fine thing. I keep mine
in a bucket in the basement. I've seen an illustration
of Pope Silvester and the devil, and Silvester seems
to be having such a nice time I can't begrudge the
fellow. What are you scribbling there?'

'I've been mapping your digressions. Here.' And
she held up the notebook – it showed a wobbly
sketch of a dolphin. 'If you continue to dissemble, I

will arrest you for obstruction.'

'You've said it precisely, Inspector. Supplicants come here caked in excuses, clogging their own honesty. Thankfully they mostly love the trappings and miss the point. Miss Shafto appeared with some young spatterbrain, a bookherd I believe he was. Hoarding wisdom till it stinks, eh? I thought I was a wise man once, then I saw one tiny ghost and was screaming like a novice. We like to think death is settled business but the bugs are busy, eh? Well the two of them stood there boneless with compromise, talking like repeater birds. I could barely get a word in. The boy arrived on some sort of snot barge heaped with apricots. The girl had at least a hundred eyes.'

'What did you talk about? It's reasonable to assume the fun didn't stop.'

'What tremendously easy riddles you ask! We talked about the suspicion that, every few years, a city's meaning is translated a little. Over centuries its very purpose could be utterly different. Children today, they're like the blot left on the eye when a thing has fled. But then they surprise you by querying a small inconsistency in a book from years ago. I told them the parable of the rope and the swan. They left with their ignorance undiminished I assure you. Afterwards I tried to evaluate the experience and decided I should laugh at it, so I did – there by the hat-stand.'

'Which book did you discuss?'

'*Darkle*, yes. Even the fools in it are floridly articulate. Open her up, see what she can do.'

'A snot barge. A hundred eyes. Laughing by a hat-stand. Who's likely to find these details plausible?'

'Anyone conversant with the outlandish discrepancies of life. Here we are, made of convoluted meat and on some sort of spree. It's a full-time job dignifying this craven mess with an explanation, Inspector. What do you think my books are in aid of? And what are you doing about the street clowns?'

'What?'

'The clowns in the street, even out here. Nothing will content them but to judder at my window. The government and its benevolent ramparts should do something about it. It's your job to depict justice isn't it? I hold you accountable. Not a week ago one appeared salivating at that window there. "Why are you drooling at my window?" I asked. "It's the very thing I like – to drool at the window!" said the clown. "That's not what I asked," I said. "Then you're complicit, *senor*, complicit! Ha ha ha!" And he capered away, all a-cackle. "What?" I shouted after him. "Don't call me *senor*! Why did you?

Why?" Well there was no reply, as you can imagine. We've ransacked the world for absolution and here we are, besieged by clowns. Proof, if any more were needed, that this country is ready for a great burst forward into blinding bloody madness. The older and fatter I become the more I suspect we complicate things when wondering at human behaviour. Seeing a harmful act and believing nobody is capable of the stupidity or ignorance it would require, we import every grand and evil motive we can dream up. Don't you believe it. Stupidity's the coin of the realm. Even fear doesn't match it.'

Nightjar sat down. 'Perhaps you've become sentimental with age, Mr Carpstein. Deliberate ignorance is a proven strategy. We've all seen someone glimpse a fact they don't like and decide not to know it, because it would mean having to be kinder or more thoughtful. Those people will pretend a cat isn't sentient so they can kick it and watch its pain. It's added value. When you make me state the obvious you demean us both.'

'I know. You're right. When an old churchbell becomes eccentric, people will say it doesn't ring "true". That's what age and texture will get you, if you're lucky. The other day I got on my knees to a duck – it's a scandal – with bread. *Bread* I was holding! I like it out here in the smalltowers. If a building's cornerstone is bigger than a man, I know it's not for me. But you can't walk anywhere without inhaling an opinion. This world's a conceit with enough detail to absorb us a lifetime, all the worse for its pain being real and quite terrible. If you're very lucky you eventually succumb to yourself. Reach a time of really owning your own bones, eh?'

'It's true life makes it difficult to concentrate. Hardly anyone does. Are you working on something these days?'

'*A Court of Steam and Otters*. The usual ingredients – an irascible magician, a wandering troubadour in a flop hat, a witch in a skin-and-bone house, a city with streets of wrinkled quartz, a giant with a fob-watch the size of a manhole cover, a one-note warlock, some world-class flames, and for continuity a tortoise. Plus a mermaid called "Plug" if I feel that way. Huddle several ideas together and they're bound to touch here and there. That doesn't mean a meaning, just a bit of conductivity. No use being ingenious anymore, is there?'

'Perhaps the fashion will come around again Mr Carpstein.'

'I don't know, a lot of what passes for goblins these days is just people bending forwards. You'll find a decade's books clog together like clay and fall away when no-one's looking. Immortality through art? Just as well bury a bottle of blood. I'm a tongue in a cage really. You see, scribes secrete their own opiate. Powerless in this annihilative abyss, we find we can arrange words and images upon a page quite freely. While we can't move the world, we move the symbols and signifiers for it. Oh the thrill, for a little while! But our words go back to common air. It helps to know it doesn't matter. I'll tell you a secret – I wanted to change the world. I've accomplished nothing.'

'Everyone returns from the Crusades a loser, Mr Carpstein.'

'Well, I'm now in my second or third childhood, they tell me. The iris of my brain won't clench to absorb what's out there. But I've found as my mind began dissolving I became more coherent to others. More on their wavelength I suppose, and the few who read me are very pleasant people, very pleasant indeed. I was born to convalesce, it turns out. In fact I believe these walls are slowly digesting me.' He stopped as though seeing her for the first time. 'You're a handsome enough baggage, Inspector. I may look like a rhino but I don't charge. Granted, parts of me are purple. Not the parts you can see.'

Out of all patience, Nightjar stood and reached for her pistol, laying her hand on the book she had pocketed earlier. She retrieved this and frowned at the cover. The title was embossed in copperplate beneath a picture of a stricken tower. *Truth's Flying Visit.* She flicked to the author page.

'I have to go,' she said quietly.

§

Nightjar's notes: Hugo Carpstein, cranky and vigorous. This discoloured gentleman is a case study in the sort of inscrutable genius whose mind begins to degrade and finally writes something accessible on the way down. He did something remarkable and spent the rest of his life in a stupor of misgivings. A man can interpret his defeats till the cows come home. At some point he went off the deep end and grew five beards concurrently, draining the life from his chin. Behind the overripe snout and declamatory style, a secretly jovial old coot besotted with the surprises of his own mind. He lives with a shadow so heavy he can barely drag it and Beulah, his black behemoth of a cat. Seems to be at loggerheads with his own belly. Nothing to do with the abduction. Everything comes back to Sophie, a woman of parts. Robeck lied to me. A new book by Emmanuel Feste?

10

An Illuminated Bookherd

All mud at the fringes, the coach stood on the dark side of Lasker Street. The horse kept craning its head around to give the supposed coachman a side-eye of rueful irony. Jonah sat high on the box seat in a rare mood of boot-buckled readiness. He carried within him a sort of sprung summer, a continually intimate heaven which could not be conveyed externally. Sophie was so dazzling he could barely hear what she was saying. 'Tom found recent deeds to four towers in Brewster's name,' she was hissing up at him while casting glances back at the pinstriped tower, 'but no schematics or listed use. Those plans are likely in these offices. This foreboding you feel is the rattling of a thin door. Safety is a sort of affliction if you're addicted. The thing for you to do now is eat your past before it eats you, champ!'

She was decked out as a sweep with a dirty face,

but still held the pink umbrella. Jonah himself was wearing a dustman's coat and a stupid hat. 'The umbrella, still?' Jonah whispered. 'Couldn't you be the coachman?'

'Without the requisite despair I'd be discovered. Here we go, Eaglet!' Sophie and Eaglet took off across the road.

The stacked storeys of Brewster Consolidated were not dissimilar, all had been painted black and a series of vertical steel struts added to unify it. As an elite tower, all rookery and escapades had been removed, leaving no option for Eaglet but to shin up one of the steel supports. He looked like a beetle wobbling up a spring onion. He was as good a snakesman as Tom claimed. When he had disappeared inside, Sophie waited a moment and then darted up the egg-white porch steps, the door opening briefly for her and closing again.

What a crew! Jonah sat aloft feeling quite chipper. If all he had to do was sit here without the horse dying he was probably alright. The sky was fine and starry. *A skyful of stars is the candour of the cosmos*, he remembered from somewhere. And he was beginning to feel the part until he noticed a policeman standing next to the cab, looking up at him.

'Get many fares at two in the morning sir?'

Jonah chucked his shoulders and indicated the sky. 'Storm like this, even the fish have red noses, eh guv? I envy fish. Can't be taught a lesson can they?'

'Storm, sir?'

'What a night to pretend we don't work under threat of starvation eh guvnor? They'll picture a magic dormouse with flashing eyes to avoid thinking about their enslavement and what they should do about it. Can't have that can we squire?'

'Magic mouse.'

'Legend has it honest work gets you ahead. Not at these prices! I knew that when you were a toffeelike newborn.'

The constable was unimpressed. 'I think you'd better step down, sir.'

'I will,' Jonah said with unnecessary belligerence. 'I'll make a day of it.' He got awkwardly down and faced the officer, smiling. He was feeling giddy. 'Don't kiss me, I've got a cold.'

'Been drinking sir?'

'Not with a head like mine,' Jonah pointed to his head. 'Have to be ready for anything with this one. Got it cranked up to ninety. It'll ruin me at last.'

Jonah laughed, but because he did not want to offend the policeman who was standing directly in front of him, he laughed from both corners of his mouth while keeping the middle closed. The effect was apparently not what he'd hoped, as the officer looked suddenly alarmed and ready.

Jonah was feeling a mixed-up joy close to panic. 'Yes, what *is* justice if it's seen by neither the perpetrator nor the victim? I know what you're thinking about, constable, but it isn't so.'

'Now sir, we both need to –'

'The truth is, yes, the truth is my soul's flaring open like a flower! I'm in love, officer! That's what it is of course! Jonah Robeck, you *are* a mooncalf!' He had reverted to his own accent. 'I'm beguiled by a fizzing wound I can't leave alone. A glutinous lozenge of refusal, worth more than gold! It's thrown me into the sweetest disarray!'

'Well it's very nice sir but –'

'Passing a churchyard, I look at one of the older graves and wonder why I ever had that ambition! The world popped open as it were, a surprise that raised the hair on my soul! My blood's gone fuzzy, buzzing! Blood!' He took some pennies out of his pocket. 'I don't recognise these coins! Help me! I'm done waiting for this dumb universe to inhale!' Jonah gripped him by the arms. 'An ecstasy under the mind! Blood!'

'Put your hands behind –'

At this moment of peril, lightning flashed twice in the second floor windows of the Brewster building, in time to the crack of gunshots. The constable paled with shock, his own barker already drawn. He stood uncertainly a moment, then at a third shot he ran toward the trouble. He was just turning to shout 'Stay there!' when a uniformed figure sprinted out of nowhere and tackled him to the ground, the two forms skidding through grit. The heroic stranger appeared to be a soldier.

§

Sophie spread the schematics over a crowded desk. They depicted four similar structures beneath the designation *Amplifiers*. At a glance each tower looked like a locked and armoured chrysalis. The head housed a drum of technicalities resembling a dry poppy's stigmatic disc.

She looked up at a sound. Eaglet was squawking in the grip of a man inked in indecipherable script. The man held the boy in one thick arm and raised a pistol with the other, his eyes like nailheads. Sophie dropped and confetti exploded over her head. The tattooed man was huge and half his energy seemed to go into navigating his very smart suit. Eaglet bit down on his hand. The man threw the boy off without crying out. Sophie popped her parasol and stood from behind the desk, the flared shield absorbing another shot, then collapsed it again and charged at the big man with its blade deployed. His gun fired into the floor as Sophie's lance pierced his belly and stuck into the wall behind him. He dropped the gun and looked down in mild puzzlement. She could see conjecture moving beneath his skin. 'What you do,' he said, and felt for the shaft of the spear, trying to get a grip.

'Don't touch the –'

The umbrella popped open and a pink mist stained the air.

Sophie and Eaglet clattered downstairs to the entrance. Eaglet pelted into the road but Sophie's path was blocked by a sturdy figure. 'Sophie! Come with me!'

'Frank! What are you doing here?'

His dress jacket was open like a blown chestnut. 'I followed you from the glass shop.'

'Must you make yourself available to every disgrace?'

'*Me*?' he exclaimed in outrage.

'Are you drunk?'

'Not so much. I'm a bloody marvel! I'll box the devil's turkeyfoot head!' And he began singing something about the hinge of a mollusc.

'Oh Frank I have to go, goodbye.'

She ran across the road and threw herself into the coach. As they set off she thought a moment, her skin numb as rubber. 'Oh, balls.' She clambered sidelong out of the carriage and on to the box seat, where Jonah seemed to be having the time of his life. 'Jonah,' she shouted over the noise, 'you can't go back to Drood Street. Frank knows you're involved and he knows the shop. He'll be telling everything to the bloody peelers. Take us saltside.'

11

The Divan of Valentine

Nightjar sat in her curved office in Caledonia Tower, absorbed in the pocket oblivion that was *Truth's Flying Visit*. She was transfixed as though by a bend of electricity.

The Inspector was familiar with the works of Emmanuel Feste, an obscurity with a sixth sense of humour who was said to have blown 'a swarm out of a whistle', shouting from one horizon to the next about how morality is not altered by altitude and annoying all by demanding that his pursuers keep up. She had seen a copy of an early handbill called 'A Fool Sells His Time'. It was a sort of fable in which something uncanny was going on. Feste's style changed after that, as if he had gained confidence and taken charge. Previously known for a sort of marauding intelligence able to bunch reality into stellar excruciations, he now spoke one truth after another under the guise of impish naivety, like a series of sensible explosions. The next little homily *Hey Bloodsucker* had explosive undertones despite its incantatory stagecraft. The book went largely unread, but for the few who witnessed the attack first-hand it gained a reputation. Nightjar had found this treasonous pamphlet in the pocket of a would-be agitator she had apprehended in Kleist's Marionettes in Third Square. He treated it like a battle bible and carried it in a luxuriously decorated steel reliquary case with intermeshing cogs in its tooled metalwork. Yet all he was doing to disturb the shop's customers was juddering in place while dressed as a farmer. She had often noticed this tendency to fetishize a book while disregarding its contents. When asked why he had done the act, he replied that it was the only possible way of expressing how he felt.

Nightjar remembered her own youthful disappointment at the supposedly seditious. She would grip the latest controversy and think, 'I hope it really *is* subversive and not another waste of time.' And she would be met with the tale of a despot who crafts an already-burning empire for the hell of it, or the tired mantra about weightless bones in a looking-glass.

Any book could be defined as a feed of words and symbols which operates a kind of sorcery. *Truth's*

Flying Visit and its intricately machined interior had a furious clarity, an ungentle wisdom sweet with spite. It was a sprint through charged absurdities into the justified resentment where god cannot follow. The idea had the unexpected strength of honey, sticky as blood outside for the first time. Giordano Bruno was burnt to death in a flower market for less. But what did it matter now, when nobody read the real thing?

Then she got to this passage:

You've been beguiled by negotiations in which no side represented your interests. When a nation decides to go to war, it first turns upon its own people. Just as the rivalries arranged in a motor can be used for any purpose, a war can be so used. War's manifold misdirection moves the money with freakish grace.

It had occurred to her that the ransom note had a similarity of syntax to the works of Emmanuel Feste, and a like concentration. The transactional feel of his tracts was like a joke in a different sequence. But this was a direct quote. A glance at the copyright page confirmed it was printed 1886, the ink still fizzing. There was no address for the publisher, Tressell House.

Nightjar summoned a young officer and told him

to find Tressell House's current address. She had to repeat the instruction several times, but he seemed to finally understand.

Far below the window, the city looked blown and open-geared.

She rode her regulation kettle car to Drood Street, where the shops were already opening. Robeck's Reflectives and the rooms behind and below it were abandoned.

She drove the bonesplitter to Percy Valentine's chambers in Shroomsbury, which also looked empty except for an opulence of ornaments all the more suspect for being unidentifiable. She tried to mentally attach a description to the furniture but it didn't all fit. Central was a giant warty gong, probably a symptom of Eastern studies. A mahogany bookstand carved like a totem pole, with the angry faces of authors. Just the sort of farfetched bargain found in an Arabian market. A plush red divan with harlequin legs. Lamps with skirts. A clockwork cello. Persian dumbbells. A bust of Pallas. Golden wallpaper scored with strange targets and a green carpet like the patterned skin of a reptile. The scent of Indonesian cloves. An imported heaven that didn't match. It had the atmosphere of a dressed theatre stage when everyone has gone home. At the rear were two ornate doors which even her skills could not penetrate, and it occurred to her that they were simply nailed to the wall. It reminded her of Sophie's apartment in Helgravia, which was lifeless as a dollhouse.

Nightjar re-emerged onto the street to find five clowns leaning against assorted facets of her car, dead-eyed and stiff as planks. Clowns, no longer paid, did it for free and were often arrested. Such tricksters had become increasingly inventive and perverse. This shower was fairly mild, but as Nightjar proceeded in a circle around the tin machine threatening a couple at a time with her nightstick, those who moved away would then return like flies when she had proceeded to the next. This went on, round and round, in silence for twenty minutes.

The Inspector was no fool. According to the Raven Method, almost anything could be used for contemplation. The average day resembled the beguilements of a ruse, and upon repetition the average fellow grew thoroughly used to it. It was adversarial and easy to predict. She herself had once mediated between a penitent and a jailer, and become crazed with the binary. Now she valued the sort of rhythmic errors that made it hard to tell how much time had passed because, properly harnessed, the hypnotic element was mentally stimulating. On her seventeenth lap around the car, a pattern was emerging in the Shafto case.

So much pointed to Sophie, whom the Inspector now pictured as a self-formulating wildcat who cut her own hair like a saint. A lifespan gone the opposite way has all the granularity of treasure. Naturally, arranging this network of suspects around Sophie had the effect of placing her at the centre of it all, and it's easy to fool yourself if you're clever. At the opposite magnification, everyone was culpable. This was rare as a crime but common as a circumstance. The trick was to set it all spinning and watch what irregularity threw it off balance.

When she returned to Valentine's apartment she found him lounging on the divan. He was in a costume like the black and red cubes of purge dice, only partially concealed by a leather bathrobe. He also had on a ruff resembling a piano keyboard and his hair was a mustard-coloured floss. He cast a dozen shadows amid all those lamps. 'Are you Percy Valentine?'

'In a roundabout way,' he drawled.

'I've no time for tomfoolery. I am Detective Inspector Nightjar.'

'I scarcely think I'm to blame for that!'

'I called an hour ago and was not received. Now you're lolling here despite not having entered by the street door. Is there a roofway?'

'Well it doesn't matter why, but I was in the bath for two hours, trying not to laugh. Alright, I'll tell you – I was disgraced awake by urine. I see by your embarrassed recognition that you've found yourself in a similar pinch, Inspector! We capsize every morning into a world without instruction, and it's all we can do to keep our masks on! What are those punctures in your nose if not to plug a mask into?'

'These "punctures" as you style them are my nostrils, as I think you know.'

'I'm parched. Is there any lamb?'

'I am a detective, Mr Valentine.'

'Hot wine? Have some tea, you'd be mad not to, in a goblet. It's called a goblet because it makes your mouth look small, did you know that? Humbug? Macaroon? A carbolic of ape's milk does wonders for the hatchet-faced. Sit down. There's nothing strange about it and the operating principle has been known for centuries.'

'I am investigating the possible abduction of Sophie Shafto of Shafto Steam and Boilers. Are you a member of the Shafto-Brewster-Sparks accord?'

'Accord! Well, they are slight acquaintances of mine, at the club. We've clinked skulls a few times. It gets dark quickly in there, especially with the door locked. Optimally I'd describe us as snotmates.'

'"Snotmates?"'

'And now you're apprehensive. There's no pleasing you, Inspector. Your procedures are voracious. The gentlemen you mention sit gruntled in occluded corners while their wallets fatten like toads in a cellar. Men of affairs. They'll put a bridle on a rose if there's money in it. I have a very weak understanding of such stuff. My family's in land. I believe my broker bought a few Shafto bonds, but it's swings and oranges. I don't know anything about it every day, and that keeps me busy enough. The ocean is unlaboured – even the spume's easy. And so it is with me. I live in the hourly midnight of ruin, thanks for asking. I lay with ten mouths open to darkness. My head is leaking into the great beyond. I'm fallen open like a book, look at me! Look at my legs!'

'Try to focus, Mr Valentine. Are you friendly with Jay Brewster?'

'We know eachother's useless names.'

'Is that the full extent of your acquaintance?'

'Well I wouldn't know, of course, but he's all sham. The fellow drains into the room like an unguessable bargain. Poking at his fraudulent furnace to keep the pretence up. Lord Shafto? Tubby fellow who tilts around like a churchbell. Imperious and boring, a bad combination. That medal he wears is actually the nose of a cougar. And as for Talion, he's a baleful old skeleton. Have you questioned him? When he can be induced to speak at all he speaks of himself in the third person as though pleading infancy. Come to think of it perhaps he has us banjaxed too. What's the saying? He "eats a trifle behind wolfskin curtains". Really they're ahoot with lies over there. I daresay an adjustment's on the cards. I anticipate a real crackerjack of an uprising. Mind you, I own a Sparks Landau and my only complaint is the static puts my hair on end. Misfortune shows me a good time – like a bad girl.'

'You make no secret of being utterly forsaken – you advertise it. Though in a somewhat frivolous and stylised manner.'

'And radiant skin, I think you'll agree. Cases like mine – I mean people with the attributes of a swan – have the foam-born effrontery to speak from the heart. Such raptures threaten to reveal an underbelly – which as you know is the worst kind of belly.'

'Your raptures are rubbish, Valentine. Even if they weren't, an eclipse never sticks, thank goodness.'

'I'll do what I can to ignore your remark, though constrained by the fact that you still stand before me, ominous as a jackdaw on a draining board.

Frame your next question with exactitude, as though putting it to a magic goblin. My face opens forward into your world. Make it worthwhile, if you can.'

She looked pointedly about the gilded apartment cluttered with arcane appurtenances. 'It's said that a fragile ego is like delicate furniture which you have to be careful around. Sell it or burn it, but don't accommodate it.'

'Don't feel ashamed, Inspector. I'm that way myself. That painting behind you, *Hog's Venice*, a clotted masterpiece discarded by one who moved on. The connoisseur will always seek out that figure in a painting who is pointing to some seemingly insignificant detail which gives us a fighting chance of finding fact amid commotion. It clues us in, you see, with a symbol? Now look at this landscape of harrowing pigments and loaded detail. A dark green skeleton poles a black gondola in the lower left corner and points at a nearby duck. Emblematic of an artist who doesn't give a red damn what you think.' He flung an arm at another stretch of tattooed wall mounted with a great flap of leather. 'And what are the odds, a stingray or a saddle with eyes? Either way it has a needy expression.'

'Are you a student of the East, Mr Valentine?'

'Yes, the mystical East. Anything's weighty when full of sand isn't it? I've been an idiot throughout the free world and regions furtherwhere. You know, certain parts of the Orient are so grim that after you're born they tape a penny over your navel. Look here – these special fruits from the colonies only really work if you seal them up in a wall for two years. But I did it and I like it. I have eaten coconuts, which are white flesh symbolically imprisoned in a wooden case. In fact Theosophy means "the land of coconuts".'

'It most certainly does not.'

'Look here at this very long spoon. I can touch the small of the sky with this. When I bought it, do you know what the merchant was shouting? "Past concerns are quaint junk. Nothing is dangerous." I can see you're delighted by this thunderbolt.'

'What you take for delight is nausea at this miasma of decoration. I don't imagine anyone is perked up by your indecipherable wallpaper or your relics of Irish tribal art. Your inanity carries all before it.'

'I have employed every resource to make my arms more bendy and, well, my dear, you see how it is.' Valentine waved his arms around like ribbons.

'What are you doing?'

'If I'm not surprised, why should you be? Society's a sorry excuse for a meaning. Arid jocularities, ash in the air and the metaphysical debauch we have for a legal system. Enclosing this emptiness is a chocolate shell depicting whatever you please. Who could foresee that some people would be dissatisfied, eh Inspector?'

In order to take a few calming breaths, Nightjar scrutinised a ginger photogram of Valentine laughing next to a dented hedge, then replaced it on the mantel. 'How well do you know Sophie Shafto?'

'She attended one of my recitations and remained quite calm while everyone else disported themselves like barn animals. Overheard by ancestors, you'd think they'd do better. At my next recitation I plan to flood the room with sardine oil. It seems there's nothing I won't do to attract attention. Ticket sales have been disappointing, as is customary. I assume you've been exposed to my teachings. Many's the man bloodied by my verse – they see my truths and simply throw in the towel.'

'I've no time for jest, Sir Valentine. Though I'm sure the illusion of influence holds shut many-a-wrist.'

'I'm content with the illusion. And gratified it is so convincing, detective. Tell everyone my next collection, *Hot Type Conflict*, will solve the world's problems once and for all. "Confession under torture; Oh drastic output!" They say I write in the elevated language of the angry chef. And at other times I'm a "menace". When people's lies about you contradict each other it's just shoddy. It adds insult to injury. Great the day when I arrive without jeering. Who knows if I understand any more than a cat looking at a candle? In any case I've adjusted my philosophy to look with more favour on my lack of success. Are you my granny?'

'No I am not your granny Mr Valentine! I am a Detective Inspector from Caledonia Tower! *Please* answer my questions! What were your movements after the ransom note appeared at the club?'

'Well, it was a day of thirty trances, and it's hard to get anywhere when your shoulders move at different speeds. I arrived back here at five in the riddance and set about throwing a party.'

'You began preparations at five?'

'Fun is a plant with a square stem. I have engineered arduous orgies and plum races. It's tiring. Contingencies accounted for and niceties observed. You have all that yet to learn, Inspector. At the appointed hour I ate a ball of salt and hung into the street screaming my poem "There Was a Hen at the Tribunal" at such a volume, everyone knew where the party was. You've heard it. It begins:

A baby bird the size of my eye.
That sort of thing shouldn't be in the sky.

The opium was giving a command performance. It won't surprise you to hear I'm plagued by seraphim. I counted ninety upended incandescences in that wall over there. Luckily, five elves corroborated my delusions. Names you would recognize. Lady Nectareen has a spaniel with a head the width of a tomato and is deathly afraid of it. With that thing in her arms she pivoted from worthy to hysterical in a fraction of an instant. What a predicament! Fabulously wealthy and no prowess! Meanwhile Sir Archy was drowning in a glutinous complex of blue gold. He arrived in splendour and left in a plague wagon. Lord Garble was drunk and entered the room with no high degree of skill, clutching onto the doorframe to withstand his own ideas. The fact that his head was invisible made it all the more compelling. I said to Marjory, "You're pretending you don't notice anything, but look at that man whose head is transparent." I had thought it was a conversation, but halfway through I saw she meant to teach me something. I punched her and I'm fairly sure I was right. As Byron said, "When a friendship is hard it's down to your colleague." Then on other days I can't touch a spud without getting squeamish. She pushed the front of her face into a one-gallon bowl of guppies, expecting what I wonder? I'm pretty certain at this moment she's forgetting the lesson for all she's worth. Drown the head, the rest follows. Unless you're a jellyfish, clenching through the sea. Heaven devoured itself in a blunt ecstasy, if memory serves. Boschian shrimp tower. Terry danced as if recoiling from his own hairstyle. We broke a zebra vase. It's broken because everything is. And the cherry on the cake was a spot of black magic. The arduous ritual for conjuring Tuesday in the middle of Wednesday. "And when we ran out of ideas, we ate the horses." Is that the quote, Inspector?'

'What quote?'

'That gong over there,' he pointed languidly, 'announced each error as I made it. In its country of origin it's called an Everlasting Coin. My blunders have reached at least the one thousand mark. It's a gift, to be so inordinately mistaken. It throws open vast spaces. And so what if we're wrong in them? But then I have often thought that if a fellow were to sustain one chosen mistake, with discipline, over many years, it might overall resemble a human life, with all its peaks and valleys and surface detail. In any case it was the jape of the season. I was numb and warm in the diversions I like best. Consequently the following morning it was old glitter, scabby and sad, and I was suffering a surfeit of the quinceys. An entitled ailment, I know. But I resolved that to restore myself I would lick the morning dew from the tower stones. Nude, probably, and loving it. To avoid catastrophe I would keep my trousers on in the evening. And that's what I did all yesterday. No lasting harm, like bread stained with beetroot. Maybe I'll tell you later what really happened. Perhaps I entered through a skylight in defiance of local by-laws. Don't tell me you've never wondered why I'm a marvel.'

'What?'

'Well I daresay you're racking your brains to discover why I'm so fantastic. You and your vaunted magnitude are a naked grab for my opinion. Granted I'm a beautiful fella. There are always tailors in my peripheral vision, and gravity does the rest. And when the roofs slide under the stars, a multifoil angel shelters me with a wing of needles. Who can blame you for thinking I'm a pretty hero? Maybe we deserve to be transitory. I will never relinquish the doctrine that confusion satisfies itself and takes a long time to clear because it doesn't want to. I hope that cheers you up? It's a vision seen while in a self-induced state of exasperation. I'm raddled with enlightenment, look at me – look at my legs!'

'Stop telling me to look at your legs, Mr Valentine!'

'When a dog is disgusted, it merely looks sullen. Me, I scream and shout. Who is the more civilized? And they have the gall to say I'm defiled by my own preferences! When I have a spare minute I'll try for the supreme disgrace, a lust beyond the means of the human body! I suppose that's what they mean by religion. Such a delicious consecration will obviously be frowned upon by the thundering herd. Which exalted horror are they worshipping these days? The last thing we need's a thumping great deity in the middle of the damage. They talk about saviours, but what about accidents? I suspect that to such a power, if it exists, we are comical, infuriated morsels.'

Nightjar's mind had been shaken into a swarm of unrelated particulates. She closed her eyes. 'I imagine god is not a prude, Mr Valentine, and everything is included.'

'Exactly. I think you've got it. Reality is not sincere. Why would it need such excess? You have the dark solidity of burnt bacon, Inspector, and I approve. If this incident shows us anything, it's that we're a thrown-chair away from revolution. I've always felt I got the wrong bones. I should have sprung for a sharper chin, certainly. I'm wistful for the days of the Troy Clown, whose golden scorn was all we could rely on. I hear the cancering of a certain northern city conspired to create an intersection of impossible angles that bent offwise and flapped vehicles and horses into ingenuously partial cross-sections of their meaning. Some of these wedges stuck together, marbled with human anatomy. You wouldn't get away with it nowadays. But if you think about it, things here are so rigid it would only take the cutest little hip-nudge to bump you into another dimension. See the lute in the corner? The protocol is you tug at a string and see what happens.'

Overwhelmed by everything in the room, their clashing significance, Nightjar was edging slowly toward the exit. 'You're perhaps just a little too young to know the Vivid Age with any clarity. The Troy Jester and his interlude of the eighteen-sixties are better in the telling than the living. You're nostalgic for a carnival king in Christmas pyjamas, who called back to a time when the original storeys were built.'

'You mean the inventive storeys, with wings and gills. Rather like the suddenly vivid strata laid down in the sixties. Before those particular aspects of reality were squared away again.'

'This pose of yours, does it prevent your ablutions? You are so exacting in your affectations, they seem rather joyless. Are you merely following orders?'

'I love order, Inspector. It has been my salvation. I have a history of fits and frenzies, and run away as a precaution against being told otherwise. I can navigate by echolocation, but it requires that I scream when I enter a room. And I can't be the only one.'

'Please, please just stop saying that and the other things! I have made a special trip from my understanding to yours hoping at least for a gaudy souvenir. I'm prepared to be deceived, within reasonable limits, and can take a joke tolerably well. But you have conducted experiment upon experiment upon my patience. You've led me by the nose for twelve minutes. Long enough for the most hellish dance.'

'Yes. Frankly I'm flabbergasted you've listened to me this long. What are you, a sausage dog? You can't arrest what you can't eat, is that the song? But a paddywagon with portholes, that's style! I'm prepared to stance alone in a boring dungeon. Or kill me, go ahead – I shan't make any difficulties. Interestingly, my brain is a helix.'

'I beg your pardon?'

'Yes, like a corkscrew descending into the neck.

I've had quite a bit of interest from the medical profession. They cast doubt on my right to occupy this species – as if it's so very exclusive!'

'I was told you only approximate a human being. Now I understand. Just above the seabed is a shifting suspension of crumbs. You're worse than that.'

'Wobbling like a noodle on the seafloor am I? Could there be a reason your disapproval holds such a complicated charge?'

'You, sir, are a dropped egg. You've been doing whatever you damn well please till you're laying there abjectly illuminated and no use to anyone. Any conclusions drawn from your frazzled scrutiny are useless.'

'To yourself be true, Inspector, at long last. All this charging around plays you false and bores me. I recommend perplexity. It casts a wide net.'

'I'll have you shovelling squid beaks in Dorset. The bursting geometries behind your eyes won't save you then.' And she threw herself out the door.

He was calling after her. 'I want you to know if the situation were reversed, I'd wear a bonnet! So you see, I can be helpful! I've pencilled in a blow of fate for 11.30! Until then I'll redouble my torpor! May you meet your fears with lidded eyes and a pet leopard!'

Nightjar reeled down the echoing stairs, her brain

fairly spuffing out of her head like a puffball fungus. She burst gasping into the street, immeasurably relieved to have escaped the chaotic confines of that conversation. The five clowns were there, smiling horribly at her.

§

Nightjar's notes: Sir Percy Valentine, a preening dandy who wrote a mock-epic poem about his arse. Another literary failure is due out next year. Counts among his acquaintances many well-born wastrels and petty poets. There is a tale of him posturing with such fervour he broke his hip. Though not quite old he seems a relic of the Vivid Age. Exhibits a sourceless merriment, blurts riddles without thinking them through and delights in an apparent puzzlement at his own revenues. I found him in a kind of stupor. Arcane calibrations on the walls. Casual outrage and excuses from the Orient. Decadent artifice doesn't have much scope. Most finery is mimicry or speculation. It tells a tale, like a bullet-hole in an accordion. As his mania accelerated he became a volcanic spurt of cryptic farce and embarrassing frivolity. Claimed he was fantastic, a wonderboy. He did not explain how he arrived at this conclusion. I was at a loss as to which aperture he was speaking from. At first I tried to accommodate his capering agitation and baffling jocularities. He started playing wild pranks with what I'd just told him, lying like mad and, yes, re-indulging the lies that were already established. Described his failings in a great deal of detail. When you stretch the truth you need to add detail or it gets thin. Did I startle him? Slipping off a cliff, a mime does some of his best work. Profundity may be taken for frippery, and contrariwise. His carefully cultivated air of irrelevance establishes the impression that you could upend his entire content without consequence – that he amounts to nothing more than an energetic discrepancy. He casts several interesting shadows, not all his own. Perhaps cunning but not in a way I recognise? The experience had something about it of my head being shredded like an onion. Valentine seems a man who deliberately runs slower than the devil, giggling as it grabs him. And if his legs are any indication, he could run much faster.

12

The Confidence Man

'I'm glad we could do this,' smiled Jay Brewster, gazing vaguely around the Skydome Tea Court. 'Now that you're cleaned up a little, I can thank you in a civilised manner.'

Lieutenant Frank Lukas looked wide-eyed at the elegant galore of potted palms, chessboard tiling and green steel furniture. The latticed ribs of the glass and iron roof threw reptilian sunlight across the leaves as clogged grandees sat in a rigid trance. A small display fountain was fringed with metal verdigris frogs.

'I do appreciate your containing that little scene and not blabbing to the bluecoats. The heart of true freedom is opportunity.'

Frank tried to clutch at this idea and found nothing but a clicking convulsion. He sensed the man sitting opposite was coated in something slick and flavourless. On the table between them was a city of silverware and a hideously carven box of apple butter.

'But really,' the Amerikaan continued, 'I don't care why you did it. A worm pinned open has all sort of detail but it's still a goddamn worm. The cop you killed will simply disappear.'

'Killed? I only knocked him out!'

'Keep your voice down, soldier! This is a classy establishment. No need to telegraph it from Kimlico to Biccadilly. Try a cucumber sandwich. Colour costs extra. You look eager and puzzled at once, like a dog at a science fair.'

'I don't know what I was expecting a "jamboree" to look like,' said Frank, 'but I don't think this was it.'

'More used to Dick's Chop House eh? Demoralized sailfish on the wall? I can see you're trying to assess the experience. Look over there.' He pointed discreetly to a desiccated dowager in a hat which looked four times divorced. 'Lady Surmise. She has a deportment so elevated that her own people have seven times invited her to leave by the window. Just behind her is Lord Albeit, dense and gutless as a gem. Baron Surge there distinguished himself by making a mistake which was foundational to modern governance. That thick-set gentleman is Viscount Green, an investor so cannily wrong he gathered a cult around him despite his disasters. Lord Balderstone, a red face and an empty skull. Lady Squelette: if there's one thing I've learned, it's that an ostrich looks the same when interrupted. The Baroness Bellifax there, who appears to have taken shelter among her costume. She wears outfits of a different colour for each hour of the day – it's called "hour cloth". Will she wear such finery in her tomb? Ants love silk. Commodore Falter is also under the influence – each of the buttons on his jacket is a working watch. Get close to him he sounds like a cricket. He seems intent on viewing you with his nostrils before his eyes. A nose goes both ways, remember. Baron Hammerquill, Lord and Lady Sudden, Squire Balderdash and Lord Underwent. They live on a schedule of courtesies and contentless grandeur – and this is them in public and their society best. Imagine how they empty out behind thick walls. Every one of those crazy hats costs you a lifetime, soldier.'

Frank looked at the armada of millinery before him. Here were carousel hats, ammonite hats, oxblood cloches, clockwork toppers and magic lantern bonnets. Stovepipes with real smoke. Boaters with sails. Hats like cakes, wicker cages, gondolas, soap bubbles. A hat which was a formaldehyde jar with something in the murk. Another recreating a sylvian scene from the baroque period. And everywhere the tall, banded toppers known as tower hats. Their wearers ate crone fruit and supped a complex cosmology of teas while appearing not to move at all. They were like a coterie of torsos in a fashion shop window.

'You've heard the fad for having a clock in your topper?' Brewster asked, arching an eyebrow. 'I heard some chinless baggage say the other day, "If a hat doesn't clang it says nothing." She had an actual belfry in her bonnet. There they are, soldier. Lords, ladies, the lowest of the low. And here you are, hot-blooded and mundane. They need a thing done and you're bushwacked by ambivalence. Bleed on their behalf and they'll sell your furniture off at three times its value. They're Tories and don't even feel the lack of it. The only warmth they have is when the tea's going down. And all of them afloat on a prearranged sea. The owning classes are flawlessly boring. Some argue it's a sort of camouflage but it isn't. They venerate a space between them where each imagines there is an understanding. And collective emulation makes for a dull show.'

'It is a little like watching a very, very boring circus isn't it?'

'They costume the moment because otherwise

they'd just be sat in a greenhouse drinking rusty water. Most lives are an attempt to beautify a mistake. So's the average empire, along a ways. Everything my people built on the erased antiquity of Amerika was denial and embarrassed haste. I thank heaven for the bird which, when Columbus thought he would never sight land, flapped onto his deck with a dollar in its beak.' Brewster smiled, pleased with himself.

The light gloomed and Frank looked up. Beyond the Court's prismatic ceiling moved a red-and-silver zeppelin heading for the Fawcett Dirigible Platform. It was probably refuelling before flying on to Biggin Airpark. 'I insist on knowing the fate of that crusher I tackled.'

'Oh, he's gone behind the scratched door to nothing. Had a nasty run-in with a baby lamb, I hear. More importantly I now need a replacement for Jack, the fellow you found on display. I've seen Sophie with that parasol. Didn't know it contained a hydraulic sword. Well I don't suppose she was forced, not that one. Whatever it is, she's in on it. I suspect, yes, I seriously suspect she's nuts. Too much reading and such turns a girl barn-sour.'

'You're offering me employment?'

'Jack was the sort of fellow who names his knives. Scrapbooked the ears of his enemies. He'd remove your jaw calm as a groom removes a saddle. Kill you at night for personal glory, attack a chef for sport, rob you left-handed to feel it anew. Ironically he was unlettered and none of us dared tell him what his ink said. We called him Schoolmaster Jack because he was barely smart enough to keep his knuckles in a row. You I'll call... the Middleman. Looking back, Lieutenant, do you ever feel you were at certain odd instants constrained to be a certain person, some artificial disgrace entirely alien to your nature, just to make a specific impact on someone else's life in one moment? And when that impact was delivered, you were freed to be yourself again, as if dismissed from the other's story? Some claim it's all like that, living life like a strange account of ourselves. It could certainly be said of you. Suppression is best done by the victim. The devil you meet at the crossroads is yourself. Average soldier, the way he's told to surround himself is a crime. A gun to pin your pants up and a lie to pin your fears on. So many went green into the fire didn't they? Admiration won't even stick when it hits a wall, and to be honoured means being set aside for special misunderstanding. Even a flounder has a sense of direction, soldier. Use your head. Or your heart. Either's better than what you're using now. You're a goddamn meat compass.'

'Is this meant to win me over?'

Brewster laughed, cutting and lighting a cigar. It was a Padre Montanelli the size of a baseball bat. 'Listen, I started out with nothing but the spine on my back. My father was a dirt-charmer who died as soon as he was old enough. I entered this mean little country lugging a carpetbag of, shall we say, fanciful devices. Found myself high and dry among a tangle of busted puppets. A small enough land that everyone's laid face-first against everyone else and determined to ignore the other. It's a goldmine. And to think you were oysted here. The idea laid its eggs in your eyes early. Oh, the White Colony'll get there, but it'll take another century. But right here and now we have thirty million liars fitted so densely together they make a smooth surface. A doctrine of stacked discrepancies is a blast for men like me. Reverse alchemy, buckaroo. Experts were quick to say I was a bastard and they may be right. You know they even blame my generators for the weather? Phantom fog and summer snow. My wife says I'm too forgiving. She's in New York now, that's why she doesn't know. Boy, Daisy can sure handle a Gatling gun.'

'Is she in the military?'

'Military?' He looked amused. 'Marriage is both a refuge and a combat zone for two. Ours is built on a thrilling acrimony. We even had the ceremony on a gangway over a turbine hall. My stars, boy oh boy! Nor do these critics of mine appreciate the planning and discipline required. Not much is achieved in one chunk, unless you're an asteroid. Look at economics. It's a thousand excuses all glued together like an insect hive. Morality? I like it marshy, a pronounced syndrome. Play bauble-chess with nations and call it the Great Game, why not? It's comforting to think we live in the interstices of a titanic bug, the nestled toxicity of that. It would explain just about everything, wouldn't it slugger?'

'What about god and country?'

The Amerikaan took a long pull on his cigar. 'God and its dog amuse each other – they haven't glanced this way in years. Fear is the optimal motivator. What else can make whole populations march backward into their own waste? Fear's a goldrush. And unacknowledged, due to the action which acknowledgement would require – that is beyond treasure because it replenishes itself through shame. Trillions of little cellular evasions, that's a battery. The energy yield is dependable and spectacular. And you can take that to the bank, Frank.'

'I'm of the opinion that to see the original facts of the world you need merely open the curtains. Or by all means close the shutters against reality – those shutters are made of the same stuff.'

'Oh those who want reality rarely want all of it. All of reality? Nothing would operate under such conditions. Reality, and the creativity that springs from it, must be limited, overtly or otherwise. Anything else is madness.'

'Why?'

'Well for one thing, our systems would fly apart.'

Frank noticed that the cigar smoke had risen to a certain height and stopped, as though there were a second glass ceiling beneath the visible one. 'Then our systems are faulty? And who decides where the limit is set? You?'

'Me, others, and the lower the better. Do you think your war could be justified on the facts? Would that airship be up there if your countrymen hadn't abducted our best sky engineer? No, as that fanatic the Rook says on his calling card, "For all the reasons you can't imagine". Now the second motive for imposing a limit, is that people prefer it that way. You could call it a trade-off but it's barely that. The word's "collusion". The acknowledgement of that would be an almighty spanner in the works, sport.'

'I can see, by the options you've presented, that you want to herd me in a particular direction. You think I have a cork mind floating on the surface of things. Or that I'm too modest to find myself?'

'No. Seems like you've been left out of your own body, is all. Any academic qualifications or other gruesome souvenirs?'

'You've guessed it – no.'

'Good. Where do you see yourself in ten years?'

'In the ground, fading like a bitemark.' Frank observed the liveried waiters who were so haughty they seemed to be going about with their eyes closed. 'I have a recurring dream of three tigers I have to take care of without any training. By sheer chance they don't kill me, though they're mirthfully aware of the option. In life I just spend a year until I arrive at another. I'll propagate myself, or something like it, maybe. That's the extent of my plan.'

'So, to you life is banked damage. Scarification. It's true that chaos won't make any exception for you. You people have become as dead men in reserve. The question is, whether you care. Understand? Care whether you live or die. And what for, I suppose. But you have youth and the reputation of an intrepid bravo. My advice: live through the sludge, buddy, and sell anything that shines. The way boys barter with beaks and acorns. In your case, sell yourself. I'll make sure you're given everything you need. It's power, the high country, here and in the territories. That's the candy banister to paradise. At this point the empire's just a polished commotion. It distracts and there's value in that, but war's a tragedy in full sunlight and that runs into money. In my country there's a fable of a frog that loses a race because a guy betting otherwise has force-fed it with lead shot. How much better if the guy had sold the lead to the frog as a foodstuff. Sure as eels eat garbage, the future's ours, my friend. With my take-charge attitude and your can-do compliance, we'll break the back of the market. We'll have a world war yet. We can all see it coming. As always, the question is whether to pretend surprise. The generators I run here will give twice the yield amid the vertices of incoherent aggression. You know, I salute you, Lieutenant. You're a man after my own principles. Dynamism without content. Zero point galvanics. That's where the power is. Such a gallant shouldn't be bowed in hunger like a kangaroo. There's a cranny for those convictions, bud. Though I admit the indications are that you could live in a cave. Question is, will you work for me or end up in a muddy field with a head like a ripped strawberry. I'm having the Luxuries of the Deep. Take a gander at this darkly compelling menu while you think about it, let it rattle around in the ol' breadbin.'

The menu was curlicued and dubious. Thorn sponge, fury cake, Boston cherries, Babylon crab, Swiss rigmarole, palaver pie, culpability stew, word salad, wing of pork, neck of merchant, hock of ghost and other blasphemies.

'There are greater profits to be made when a war turns catawampus,' Brewster continued thoughtfully, 'but you need men on the ground, amid the chaos, making deals in the moment. And an evolving destination may disappoint – slips out of register, you see. That's where fascism has the upper hand. Fascists live in a simplified description, one which is easy to conclude. It's about the last say. They're like children in a way. "Fascism? Take me to the railing and tell me what to shout." Considered as a group they don't make sense. As individuals they evoke pity. It's short-lived but by god, a powerhouse for those with the smarts to harness it. I might try it out when this place runs dry. What are you having?'

'The pilotfish. And I accept your offer. You seem a dependable man.'

'Then the illusion is complete. Spit on your mitt and it's binding. Relax, young man. It's not your lucky day.'

13

A Strange Awakening

Jonah had a dream in which all was adjusted and redefined. Even the places had different names. He was left laughing and sobbing before a wall of burnt sugar, then found himself seeping awake in a sailcloth hammock strung across the weather deck of the Custom House. It was the strange and pleasant sensation of arriving on a new foundation. A dirty seagull was screaming at him from a junction box planted with flowers. He staggered up through his fuzzed-out senses and squinted down at a half-tide stuck with rusty ribs.

The candied sensation of that dream haunted the morning, and he tried telling Sophie about it. Intoxicated by proximity to the ultravivid stickiness of her brain, he was riding his heart with no hands. 'I've had a banquet of sleep. I feel renewed, for once.'

Sophie was in serene good spirits, standing at the

shack's stained window. 'What a lovely sky! Get a good look before the detail stretches!'

'As I nodded off I knew I was coming in hot, storming into sleep with a purpose. I had a dream I'd died and was chatting with a cherub at some sort of heavenly turnstile. "I'll deny you everything troublesome," it said. "Are you sure you won't find that boring?" And I replied, "Knowing what I know now: definitely not. A thing doesn't have to be troublesome to be interesting. And as you're aware, I'm exhausted."'

Sophie laughed. 'I'm glad it met with your standards, Jonah. "To dream is to speak of a planet behind its back." Some dream in English, I suppose. I dream in a language I don't understand. It isn't Dutch, I know that much.'

'So what happens now?'

'Consequences,' she said. 'You seem surprised by the idea.'

'Well so far it's been such an inchoate insurrection I can't tell if it's succeeding.'

'I know. Our philosophy is almost new, often wrong, and lives in the sea if it has to. Officially we're merely fanatics. By those lights a man who struggles when drowning could be called a rebel. A sin shouldn't be so bleak, should it? Resistance can be moral, and acceptance evil. At this point it's not even my fault anymore. Or theirs. An interesting world, but it's not easy, and it's not finished.' As she gazed outside, Jonah saw that the pupil of her eye was a little twist of fizzed danubes. In his mind he was going holy all over her. 'History repeats like bananas and we still fake surprise at the flavour. I was told repeatedly that's how it was, but finally yielded to my own faculties. Politicized governance is a galleon in a bottle. It doesn't operate in the free world. Liberty in vacuum is not quite an experience of freedom and nor is liberty in chaos. This current age has rather cleverly combined the two in some way I can't understand.'

'Well, it can change. It's been otherwise before. The Vivid Age seems to have been one of those warm corners in time, an untouched adjunct where thoughts and feelings were allowed to happen.'

'The thing about the past is it seems resolved and tied with a bow. But for those living at the time it was probably incoherent, like our present. Tom's old enough to remember. They didn't know what was next. So even they were beholden in fear. It's easy then to hook us by the tripes. Or assure us the truth is sequestered in such peculiar dimensions we'll waste years looking for the door. All for some disembodied redemption, judged by those whose pretence at classicism is craven. The state imitates religion for very particular reasons, Jonah. All I know is I kneel and thank almighty god for the black market.'

'What are you blathering about?' Tom Dollivar entered the angled room, all got up as a normal man and carrying a Gladstone bag.

'We were saying life's a real diamond of a headache.'

'Well I just had a visit from that inflated vultress Beatty Nightjar. You didn't mention her hair was shaped like a top hat and she's built like a boiler. I thought I was being nibbed. Had to pull out all the stops. Adopted an articulation so elevated it was irrelevant to her. Trouble at the office?'

'Some sort of guard. Dead I'm afraid. My umbrella opened in his belly. He's quite exploded. How was your survey?'

'You know how from one angle I look like Napoleon and from another a stupid shed? Look at this.' He started pulling books out of the bag. 'Betty Pikestaff's *Five Hopeless Senses*. We all know it as a chronicle of Betty's misadventures in Gujarat, where finally some ne'er-do-well tiger feasted her to the ground. It was completed by her husband, who couldn't keep his mirth entirely out of the account. Now I open the same book and find that an old lady irritates Cerberus so much on the way into hell that it kills her, causing an administration foul-up and all manner of hilarity. See how the cover looks like it's made of marzipan? And this thing, *The King of Red Roar Fields*, used to read like the provisions of a will. Dead exposition and lists of furniture. Now listen: "A ladybird the size of a tortoise. The apocalypse is at a tricky stage, alien trinkets clogging up the sky. But I rectify dinner, as a thousand times before, and all emerge unscathed. Foam everlasting." Hear that, Jonah? Foam!'

'Foam can indicate... well, anything,' Jonah said thoughtfully. 'Frazzling glory or a fallback for the uninspired.'

'Next, *The Stupid Spyglass*. I read this when I was a child. The essence of the story was simple. The infernal viscera of the universe poured out of the sky and drowned everyone in fire. Now it's about a boy who plays a trick on himself and ends up on the moon.'

'It's the same idea pointing in a different direction, surely?'

'Here's *The Book of Counterclaims*,' said Tom, ignoring Sophie's remark. 'I happen to know this is about a recovering deacon who finds that his forehead is made of glass. I now find it's all about a butcher who is visited by an angel with the head of a honeybee. Worse still, my own works as Percy

Valentine are beginning to fluctuate, which is a threat to my guise as a trivial mediocrity. Listen to this: "Infinity fizzes in a needle's eye. I will freeze and you will fry." That turned up in the middle of a poem about bored dogs. No, I won't have it. That spurting fount of cryptic farce and idiocy is priceless. I stand around being garishly eloquent and people make their assumptions. Do we have the plans at least?'

'Yes,' Sophie told him, laying tattered blueprints on the table. 'Though rather shot up.'

The ragged schematics even looked diabolical. Four tall spires were each configured with a watchtower housing something like the radial seedhead of an opium plant. Jonah felt deliciously included as they discussed plans in this rotten cradle over everything – an obscure glory all the more heated for being hidden.

'So he has the offices,' Sophie enumerated, 'with his residence in the penthouse. He has his power station, and then these four towers. Jewel, Stave, Stackhorn, Terminal. All the same except Terminal Tower which has a much more complex crown. I think it's the command station, linked somehow to the others.'

'I'd say it was about wireless communication,' Tom mused, 'but Brewster has never been interested.

He'd like everyone isolated in their own little vacuum jar. But if we're working on the theory that Brewster has erected denial amplifiers at the cardinal points of the city, what does that actually mean?'

'It means he's leaning into us,' Jonah ventured. 'Push people where they want to go, using their own fear. It's like a bell jar, as you said, Tom, tamping everything down. But that suppressed energy has to come out somewhere. Isn't that the whole principle of denial generators?'

'If I'd known all this before,' Sophie declared, 'I would have abducted Brewster's wife in the normal way.'

'As I've stated,' Tom said, 'I believe she's a way in. There's a lot of flam with Brewster but behind the cowboy he's an Actualogist, and so am I. We differ only in what we do with reality.'

'I daresay everyone believes themselves an Actualogist. Tom is always right and feels it very cleanly, don't you darling? You think that wisdom is insulation. But it's completely permeable, that's how it works.'

'On the contrary. I'd be frightfully slowed down if I thought there was something to be learned from each of my errors. Look for me in the infinite reaches of my mistakes! The best joke looks in every direction at once. And they say angels are covered in eyes. For all the reasons we can't imagine, eh?'

'And that's not much,' Sophie laughed.

But upon hearing the paraphrase, Jonah had experienced a realisation. 'You two are the Rook,' he said.

'Yes, we are that damned elusive Rook,' Tom announced. 'Have you only just worked it out? A plausible rogue. It's traditional that the best clowns demoralise.'

The Rook was said to have kicked a hereditary peer into a bear enclosure. Other reports detailed a figure bucking naked through Rubicon Square on a giant copper termite, but there were only ink sketches to illustrate it. 'That rampage of yours remains the gold standard for carnage round here. And your intervention at the Gram Exchange.'

'Yes,' Sophie frowned in rumination, 'three baby elephants can do a surprising amount of damage. But it was only a distraction. Tom was at the Mint, copying plates.'

'A sunset on their currency!' Tom cried. 'Take the lie by the handle and hit them with it! Sophie's idea.'

'Your taxes ensure you are indirectly complicit in a thousand crimes. Yes, without really having to think about it. War's not the pernicious fiasco many believe – it is a very successful commercial venture for somebody. Remember what happened the other times?'

'We've heard nothing through the press about compliance.'

'Father becomes strangely imaginative when he's angry. Some chain breaks in his mind and he says extraordinary things. It makes me wonder if he's still a colourful fellow, inside. In any case it's better such outbursts are not reported.'

'Ah we're floundering around,' said Tom fiercely, slamming a hand on the plans. 'The juddering clowns on the street are more organised than we are. Honestly if we fail to finalise this uprising we'll look like fools. What's the plan? Keep paying taxes as you say, until they despair of catching us out? On guard and thinking that's a solution? The age of mad masters will not reach a natural end because it hadn't a natural beginning.'

'I don't need more sermons on Rookery, Tom. I wrote them, after all.'

'Yes, of course. It's a shame. Tomfoolery was shaping up to be an outstanding approach. I even lectured a dog – see this scar? The problem with issuing an ultimatum is you may discover the truth of the situation, but really what do we have left?

Let's do something right for a change. A thing destroyed in a different order than it was created reveals new angles, anyway.'

'This isn't going to be your typical exploit,' Sophie told them, indicating the four towers. 'They've all been swept, so we enter at street level. Continuous inner stairs. We don't have a proper floorplan, just these cross-sections, but it's enough I hope.'

Tom was already pulling on some new dunnage. Along with a postman's uniform he was wearing a sloped topper like the prow of a locomotive. 'Got it from Needle & Notlove. Don't know what it means but it's the best I could do. I'll stick a badge on and wear some bloody great cog glasses. And then this blazing green frock coat over the top of it and a yellow silk cravat, like so. How do I look?'

'Like Champagne Charlie,' Sophie decided.

'Jonah, my dear fellow – help me.'

'More than anything you resemble a parrot.'

'There – see how I trust you?' Then Tom took him aside confidentially, 'Can I have a private word with you out on the drawbridge? I have something very particular I want to discuss.'

Jonah had always felt precarious and his mind had supported the feeling. He communed with particles of himself and could recite his own misgivings to nine decimal points. Now it seemed his compendious spectrum of worries had congealed together and fallen off. He had indulged escapism before. This wasn't that kind of happiness. This was a swoon which left him golden and sick. A heavenly weight of consequence. He followed Tom outside onto a deckle-edged gangplank hung ten storeys over an alley of mud. Leaning on the rail, they could see a wedge of Lasher's Wharf, the chocolate brown river and some bits of dirt which were boats. Above them the sky looked rich as a potion.

'So how do you see the current setup, young man? I have a reason for wanting to know. A reinforced relic presumably.'

'When I was young. More recently a zigzag sprint between others' demands. I know I state the obvious but you can lose yourself in others' excuses – it makes up the average life.'

'Yes, for many years I myself was anxious to discover some clear defence of the prevailing position, but never found it. The arrangement seemed merely to be a scattered assortment found at the tail-end of some long chaotic frenzy. I entered the world covered in blood – knowing Earth as I do now, I'm surprised I evaded arrest.'

Jonah watched Tom as the anarchist lit a cigarette and began to savour it. It occurred to him that Tom was actually a rather conceited fellow. Overhead a red-and-silver aerostat banked out of a deepness of blue vapours, heading for the Fawcett spire. 'That's the *Torrentius*,' said Jonah, 'of the Moorcock Line.'

'Oh? How fast does it go?'

'Fast? Maybe you value haste a little too much. Speed can be dangerous. For instance this tactical prolapse you have for a plan is ill-considered and dicey.'

'Only if something gets in the way, I should think. I'm beginning to realise, why waste time building up to a thing? You either mean it or you don't.'

'The ponderous response of a lion may accelerate quickly, as needed.'

'I suppose a man must be allowed to laugh at a thing before admitting it's inevitable. Do you realise how restricting it would be if people took me seriously? But Sophie's right, though she's mean. Don't tell her I told you. Quicksilver breaks and rejoins and so do we. To love something so completely is to love it when the colours don't have a name. Yes, to fall so long you forget you're falling. That's life, brother. And there's no villain waiting in the wings, I tell you – the entire cast is on stage at all times.'

'You can be oddly reduced when you symbolise something to people,' Jonah observed. 'They forget you're a person.'

'Yes, to be known by one's acts – you'd think this would be the most direct course to being understood. But people, if some part of them desires, can find a million ways to misunderstand the simplest thing. Then a final fight in a grain silo and Bob's your uncle. Or a cable car.'

'Bob's a cable car?'

'Final fight in a grain silo or on the bloody roof of a cable car – try to keep up, there's a good fellow.'

They looked over the shabby realm of rooves and the shacks and gantries strung between them. Spires, turrets and platforms created a sequence of details like a battle. 'Looks like a world built entirely of trapdoors doesn't it?' Tom remarked. 'But from certain vantages of roofland you can still look down on the city and see a promise amid the folded snags. It's not just a stellate segmentation of class as the anarcho-minimalists would have you believe. Sometimes in the rain a drain-hat glitters like a penny, and you feel the momentary spangle of a lost idea. Maybe the whole thing needs a substitution cipher or decoder grid laid over it. Your philosophy's a schematic lament. Might it do the trick do you think, or would it need a deity to explain it?'

'In my experience,' Jonah told him, 'nothing sticks for long. An ideal is rather like this spider, the black bead of its body full of ink. It's only when flattened that it makes a mark.' He flicked the critter from the railing. 'Then it's useless.'

'Let's just agree a city is a catastrophic result nobody had the decency to clear away. Endless blue terror keeps the birds occupied, at least.'

'That's very like poetry. You really allow that this poisonous globe could be a god's doing?'

'I know that mistakes of this scale generally require large resources. But what you call god is a blind creative impulse – a thing so far from personality it might as well be called physics. And god is everywhere, comrade. God is at the tip of my cigarette.' He took a deep drag, flaring the end.

'Then why use the word at all?'

'Why indeed.'

'It seems to me if this were a universe of blind chance, we would occasionally blunder into good fortune. How to explain the one we inhabit? Some believe it's an obliterating vortex quite sensitive enough to know the value of what it destroys, but how could it be?'

'I did not say blind *chance*, Jonah. And as for poetry –' he took a last drag – 'get it said and walk into the sea.' He pitched the cigarette into space.

14

Transformer

Nightjar emerged through a pergola into Talion's roof garden. She had had no idea this frazzling paradise existed at the summit of Sparks Tower. It was an estate scribbled with ivy and walled like a monastery yard, its few embrasured windows looking out into empty air. The pulse of a fountain, a large lemon oak, a mosaic of a dolphin, and sunfire itching over every flower. The spread was infested with nature's favourites, many of which would be better off elsewhere. Thumbflowers, lava flowers, rampion, goat roses, crab apples, tea roses, tea apples and crab roses, all in friction amid coloured shadow. Voltaic yellow tulips and poppies like a coral reef. In a corner bulged a large topiary bush representing Talion's skull-like head. Talion himself was down on claws and knees amid crowded vegetables, his coat as dirty as a banknote. This bargain of mixed bones and viscera looked not a little ghoulish.

'Baron Aksel Talion,' Nightjar announced firmly. 'I am Inspector Nightjar. Don't get up. I am at the end of my limit, so answer my questions cleanly and honestly. And spare me your life story.'

'Poor Aksel Talion!' the old man began, waving his arms theatrically, and it was all she could do to refrain from booting his face in. She had been told about his use of the third person. Lord save us from codgers who try to be cute.

'I see,' said Nightjar with a big, heavy outbreath. She looked out across the spiked city. 'I see how it's going to be.'

'I was merely going to say that impurity is subjective, Inspector. Is soil impure?' But he was no longer looking at her, nor acting out. He dug in the ground with a trowel. In fact he seemed to be in a transport of indifference.

'I'd no idea you were a student of petalurgy.'

'Well, I have a love of systems and a horror of empty repetition. That makes nature the sweet spot. Tragic that nature needs pampering but it does up here. I spend days getting the better of a snail. Vegetation and its fickle calories surround me. Nature is looping to my satisfaction. Currently it's summer, you can tell by the bees.'

'Yes. My role today is to see if I can tempt you

into breaking your silence regarding the kidnap of Sophie Shafto.'

'That dukklehusset? Perhaps I took her and she's buried under our feet? The soil is deep enough for a body, I assure you. Plurals herd poor old Talion into numerous crimes – does that count?'

'You're in competition with Shafto Steam for the war account. That's motive.'

'Yes, war – hardly a salutary trick but a profitable one. It's a horror I lack the means to enjoy, though Sparks Enterprises is an old hand. I prefer all the tickling animosities among garden pests. Every second counts when you're disintegrating. Look over there. Red daffodils are an interruption – and a welcome one.'

'Is Brewster capable of abduction? If the question doesn't violate your cabal.'

'A secret society's just a tacky casket for a question mark. As for Jay Brewster, he can't decide if he's an engineer or an alienist. He has the conscience of a starving wolf and is quite ready to make radical changes to others in order to feel secure.'

'Why tolerate him? Does he have something on you?'

'What could anyone have on such a flimsy fellow?'

'A lifetime.'

'I'm younger than I look. I'm sure you've heard about the transformer accident. As for Sophie, she never struck me as the type to remain in bondage.'

'She may have fallen under a complicated influence, or a simple one. Opinions differ. I think it's political.'

'When you make something simple it either eliminates the truth or gets to fundamentals. It depends on the motive of the person saying it.' He looked at her, his face grey as a dead nest. It was a face which had lived through nine seasons of fatality. 'Yes, just as dedication to a cause can be limiting or provide focus, depending on what compels you to get involved. You say young Sophie may have been catechised by a troubling crowd?'

She settled like a new grave next to him. 'Possibly. A revolutist can only alter what she finds. It's a tragedy from the off.'

'If the answer is nearer to the ground than the question, that usually means it's a good one. An idea's real when you can grow grass on it. Or hair. Yes, you can stamp on revolution as one might a mushroom, and the fungal kingdom does appear fragile – but underground it's always connecting in limitless profusion. Reality is quite thorough. Subsoil isn't subterfuge. Everything's included – a snail with a brain the size of a raindrop could tell you that.'

'Everything's included,' Nightjar repeated thoughtfully. Where had she heard that before? 'I have to say, Mr Talion, you surprise me. I was led to believe you were a croaking, incomprehensible wreck.'

'Croaking has much to commend it. People either lean away, or lean in, and that tells Talion a great deal.'

'What do you make of Percy Valentine?'

'A land-rich harlequin, all languid affectation and groundless merriment. I know by now how little sense there is to that hoodwink and it has never been within my gift to listen to gibberish. Talking to him's like waving at a bucket.'

'I spoke to him earlier.'

'More boring froth?'

'Fluffy as a pantomime bat. Though even a wastrel has a certain symmetry if laid out correctly.'

'There you go, Inspector, finding bones amid blossoms. I don't envy you holding strangers to account in a land where precision is a liability and continuity an embarrassment. The apocalypse at your very elbow, and every day. As a mindbearer you must be in agony. Do you get much help? No?'

'My colleagues sit transfixed by speculation. Jumping to conclusions is their only mental exercise. They've forgotten the start of a sentence by the time they reach the end of it.'

'Talion thinks an obvious motivation for forgetfulness is fear of reaching a personal conclusion. Something that may have to be acted on. Better that everything's fractured into bits, eh?'

'On top of the antiquating effect of encountering the same ideas over and over.'

'The ancient astronomers saw celestial gears and pulleys. The gears of infinity inevitably involve some duplication I suppose?'

'When I began this inquiry I wasn't prepared for the sheer gale-force ferocity of the lying I would encounter, nor its ceaselessness. There doesn't seem to be a quota to reach. I feel increasingly that I'm searching for an activity which cannot be described. How good a detective am I to dislike the world for failing to provide the facts I require? To need it to be what I want?'

'Yes, why pin labels on a thing that's always growing? Scientists think a seed is nature revving up for a tree. Every time I try for immediacy, it's instantly out-run by nature. It comes from the automatic side of immortality, which is running irrespective of our actions. The heart gulps eighty times a minute. The peaches are buzzing in the trees. Sandwiches for all.'

Nightjar could see how the neatness of coerced nature could be a tonic, for those with the money. 'It's come to my attention that your son Harry hasn't been seen for some time – he travels abroad?'

'He was disturbed by the accident,' was the rather ambiguous reply. 'It affected him greatly.'

'He was there when it happened?'

'Dealer's choice if he got the best or worst of it, detective. I don't know what to call the situation. I suppose the inevitable happened: everything we deserved.'

'That's hardly inevitable, in my experience.'

'Chemicals and elements. Be careful when handling the essence of a thing. Creation cloaks things in appearance for a reason. And voltage has a flavour, it turns out. I knew instantly that this tasted wrong. Aksel Talion died in that accident. And since then I've been living through his teeth.' Talion unfolded all his bones and stood like a fragile ladder. There was something about him of botched taxidermy. 'In one hour my nurse will be bringing me a pilchard oozing with all that a pilchard contains. I live a circumscribed life, Inspector. That's the green stuff, you see. My chin alone is valued at four hundred pounds. It's worth anything you like, look at the thing.'

'It certainly is hideous. For some reason I'm afraid for you, Baron.'

'Don't bother, I can manage that myself. And nowadays my downfall is pretty meaningless. I intend to die resplendent in my own sputum. And innards, if the fates allow.'

'For my part I pray my last-ditch hour features fierce flames and wailing women. None of your insufficiency.'

'I like you, Inspector, despite what you take me for. Look through the window here, the view is packed with distances.'

Nightjar peered out at the cramps and escapes of the city, the tangled suspension of shacks and gangways infesting the rooves like flies on a steeple cake. The towers' mismatched storeys and bands of colour resembled the unplanned play of a child.

'What's the meaning of such a confection?' Talion asked. 'Yes, the storeys are different colours and there's a flourish or two, but the towers grew as they did because people started building and that repeated for generations, always in one direction.'

'You'll find it's basic practice to build over an established foundation,' Nightjar stated, puzzled by him. 'And would you have our countryside clogged with cottages?'

'You have a point. Though I don't think that was the motive for the towers.'

'What then?'

'Trudging imitation. Thankfully we seem to be running out of steam. And the top couple of floors have no colour or flash at all, have you noticed? Not a bang or a whimper. Self-similarity determines that we repeat the same mistakes at smaller and smaller scales until we reach a point, or several.'

'A point.'

'A point where we disappear into our own scintillated dullness, of course. These disputes will last like cobwebs on old iron, Inspector. You must give up any notion of understanding it. Look at that bridgefly there.' He pointed at an insect with a gelid head. It sat unmoving on the wallface. 'You've heard those fables about people who go to live in fairyland for years, a realm where time moves differently? They return to our world with accelerated speech like the chirping of insects and move in buglike jerks. Time is outrageous, hiding and revealing everything. There are people in Asia who live for hundreds of years. At a certain point they simply stop talking, and I can't blame them.'

'If it's all so opaque, what have you learnt?'

'The limits of vitality when going in the wrong direction.' And indicating that the experiment was over, he pointed back at the door.

§

Nightjar's notes: Aksel Talion has been a powerhouse since he rose to prominence in the Association of Electrizers. A nasty nip from a high voltage wire gave him a glimpse of his own motive current and his body has never unclenched – he reportedly became withdrawn and established the philanthropic Sparks Foundation to educate on the safe use of voltaic energy. I expected a smashed brain enrobed in cranial slime in the usual style, dwelling ruefully on his more baroque mistakes. Instead I found a placid gentleman amid the beaks of lionheart poppies, tortoiseshell tulips and roses grey as sharks. A grey rose may be young or old? Talion's face raises more questions than it answers. A man clocking in at sixty years who looks over a hundred. During our brief exchange I encountered neither jagged temper nor the exhausted want of delicacy often found in the careworn. Implacable as a holy hermit, who knows what was on his mind? His head's like a stone – start peeling it I'd be there all day. His pretence at senility is probably defensive. Is Brewster more than a huxter selling leather in a can?

§

Talion loved his garden. There was a similar motive to that of the Inspector – tangible numbers and everything precisely appointed. But around that moved the great and sweet design of summer. One flower resembled a god turned inside-out like a glove and another had the subtle structure of a blessing. Grass green as clean holly. *There's no facing down a cabbage*, he reflected, still gazing out of the narrow stone window. *It won't even know I'm there. Cut it and you get a frozen chaos.*

'Hey little fella,' said a voice behind him, and he turned to see Jay Brewster emerge from behind the topiary head and stroll toward him over the lawn. 'I know what you're thinking: why enter a garden looking snazzy? I'm entitled to relish my own entrance, mister. I almost collided with that walking stave church. You had a conversation like it mattered. What did you tell her? I thought she was going to kick you at one point.'

'How did you get by my security?'

'I paid the toll. Surprisingly high. They'll have to deny it when the time comes.'

'Where is my nurse?'

'Cooking something that looks like Bastille stew, plus a loaf with a tremendous wingspan.' He looked negligently at the borders. 'A rose the size of a lettuce eh? Good boy. And what's that, cornsalad? And a potato. Don't make the mistake I made and hammer it into paste. Is this a banana plant? I guess anything goes around here eh? Those fountains with the stone fish spurting water out of their mouths – is that an event people find attractive with real fish? You have workmen to do the real gruntwork of picking flowers I assume.'

'The ribeye roses are doing well,' said Talion cautiously. 'And the trumpetflowers. The unusual weather helps on occasion. I hope there's not more snow on the way?' This last he added blandly.

'Flowers are the gobs of nature or something, don't they say?' Brewster continued, standing next to Talion and surveying the garden. 'Big deal, leaf displays. "Bejewelled mud, birds' unchecked power and the unstoppable deathray of the sun," that's what Verne says isn't it? Air surrounds us like an army. Insects are natural gadgets, triggers going off all around us. An insect – whose eye is a speck by the way – would say you'd worked yourself up into a towering doubt lately.' He peered through the stone window. 'No chance of falling through one of these, eh? More like a thing to fire arrows from. I can see the Machine Mile from here, and that elongated dome I suppose is the railway terminus. Yes, of course it is. A town stuck through with towers and a stabbing under every gas-lamp. Hardship, the best there is, and a populace whose vision of heroism is to battle through advertisements to the truth. I love it here, you know that? I can bite in any direction and get someone. I heard a fairytale once of a simple hell where demons walk arm-in-arm and dissenters wriggle in hot lava. Heard anything about that? I doubt it's much of a deterrent for them whose kids are nippers in the foundries. A tunnel of stings isn't encouraging. I was talking to a young soldier this morning. His mind wanders amphibiously in and out of others' opinions. Never stood a chance. Another card to play. Jobbing killer for the campaign. Thinks he's out of the frying pan, working for me. These people are amazing. Evasion is like food and drink to them. By god the undisturbed potential in their gormless, determined faces. So many things they dare not know. The few who use their minds are hung yelping in a sideless abyss. Who would have thought the denial of common sense could have such compelling power?'

'Zero admission energy,' Talion scoffed weakly. 'Aksel Talion put no stock in nonsense, even when everyone was buying it.'

'Tell it to the bees, kid. His stubbornness was a palace of scar tissue, not the courage you believe.

You've grown old since, the best decision you ever made. Dressing in clothes the colour of custard. Even I was gulled for a moment, wasn't I? In nature the source of offspring are quickly redundant. Not with you. To lose a father like that? You never told me where you buried him. Is he here?'

'I can never save my father. But I pity the man who enters a garden looking for something to disagree with.'

Brewster went through the motions of understanding him, then pointed at the topiary skull. 'I've been in his head, Harry,' he chuckled gently. 'He understands the utility of our deal. Someone has to be the dark meat in the family, am I right?'

'I believe I've done everything you asked of me.'

'Your role is to mumble like a gnome with a luxury amnesia, living on owl milk and dark honey. Way off the books. I can't have you blabbing to a flatfoot – not one who listens.'

'Did you abduct Sophie Shafto?'

'I didn't take that spoilt brat and whoever did can keep her. I don't care if steam's out of the picture, why would I? Denial in a war, that's perpetual motion, buddy.'

'I know very well how your devices work!' Talion snapped suddenly, annoyed with himself. 'And that they do work! The fact is my own voltaics yield more energy when weaponised. In combat my systems become hybrid without my having to make the slightest adjustment.'

'On account of people pretending to believe the propaganda? And then killing everyone as they like to. Sure, I can see that. Now think about how it enhances my system. But I need to strike now. Empire and its dream of terminal plenty, it'll bite us in the butt one day. The great ideal in a stupor of treacle-coloured cogs, and then self-sabotage by right of conquest, remember? So I need to know right now, for good and all, if you'll sign off on my scheme and withdraw your own or if you're determined to stick with Shafto in the eighteen-goddamn-fifties.'

'There's a saying: "A plant moves by growing. A person grows by moving." The man who said it had less sense than a metal toy. Here, I can sit by my own side like the wealth of an angel. We'll all have a reconciliation with the soil, I believe.'

Brewster sighed heavily. 'Unwise, Harry, like waiting in a cauldron. Has the wind up here so distracted your wits that you don't know what's practical? You can grow a moon on a post but you're glamoured by dirt.'

'I have asked you not to call me that.'

'It doesn't matter now. The town's still waiting

on an official announcement but you're toast, old fellow.' He very casually levelled a decorated steam pistol with a pearlite grip. It was as broad as it was deep. 'You've been industrious. Time for a rest.'

Talion cowered like an old man.

'Oh, come – you're dead in the future, the past – why not now? Everybody dies. It's not a skill. You can fall backward into it.'

Talion had twisted against the wall. 'You need a gun of that power on this skeleton?'

'It's visceral and it meets my needs. Be grateful. You're dying on my dime. We better get started.'

15

An Inconvenient Death

Tressell House Editions was based in the basement of Rampart Tower. It was like a cave and contained a chaos without much appeal. A printing machine like a locomotive engine was rolling on empty and sounded like a theatrical thunderboard. It was surrounded by wallpaper sheafs and unbound spuffs of abandoned books. Propped in the corner was a whalebone oar amid stacked numbers of the reformist periodical *The Lace Trumpet* and the defunct journal of sarcastic architecture *The Sidestair*. A single Talion light hung over the ruins. The smell was a mix of cloves and spent sulphur. Next to a stepladder-to-nowhere stood a sweaty man with helical hair, clad only in a leather apron and steam goggles. Battered as a sandal, he seemed to be in a wretched, hectic state which made him giggle at odd moments.

Nightjar realised she'd interrupted a scenario so

complicated she would do well not to address it.

'I keep her on the boil!' the man shouted. 'It comforts me!'

'Shut it off!' Nightjar shouted, showing her badge, and he went to throw a lever.

Mounted on the wall was a circus bill like a tea-stained reproach assemblage – it depicted three emblematic apes looking angry with disappointment. There was a Latin motto meaning 'born, cheated, buried'.

The man returned to his starting position, still shouting. 'The vibration of the modern machine shakes up the mind and heart so they become mixed and combined, can you imagine?' He punched a stack of yellowed almanacs so that they slipped pathetically to the floor.

'I need to contact Emmanuel Feste. Answer me, if you can, in Albionese and at your earliest pleasure.'

'Feste, yes!' the man yelled happily. 'What do they say, "Howling through the head of a needle"! Dogma! Like a trinket on the seashore, it shines with colour – brought home it seems dim and mundane! But by that time I've got the money! And lucky for me it's a doctrine so clotted with obstructions it can be discarded all of a piece! The next sound you hear will be me elaborating on what I just told you!'

Nightjar waited for a while but the man was just bent forward and jigging in craven exhilaration.

'The badge I showed you was intended to indicate I am an officer of the law.'

'One of the Queen's own bullies, I know! I could print you a better one! We ran a good game in penny sensations here, detective! An honoured line of fictional snoops from Dupin and Burton to Petrovich! One works by a soup of connotations and another by a collage of procedural blunders, or the science of eventuality! Road will meet hedge and so on! Humourless constable calls on well-to-do household and reveals guilty subtext! Pistol under belljar! Denouement in the library, where everyone sits for the menacing skit! And of course the monkey genre, where it was all done by a monkey!'

'I suspect there is no point denouncing a monkey. It doesn't care and you won't persist. As for the big reveal, it only works if the conclusion is less than obvious. Or everyone agrees to pretend so.'

'That's theatre, isn't it?' the feverish man bellowed. 'What's the saying about "a key and a strangler"? We had some distinguished authors too! I had the honour of publishing one of Mrs Gaskell's minor works, *Interrupting Lizzie*! It's interesting for the fact that the omniscient narrator is several times discovered by the book's characters, squatting in a cupboard or listening from a laundry basket! Have a humbug, detective!' On an upturned crate a penny-candy jar was filled with black and white. He knocked it crashing to the floor. 'Can you guess why I did that? Strap a saddle on a crab and think again! And the works of Percy Valentine! Trying so hard to be special he disappears, just squirms into nothing! Beware the man who refers to his own opinions as "epiphany seeds"! His verses are the literary equivalent of making a run for it! Being brisk and staccato can pass for humour until a prudent man speaks! Are you in the market for wallpaper? Something in a question-mark motif, repeated on the oblique?' He showed her a dented sample. 'This motif is meaningless but everybody loves it! I call it Baritone Meadows! Look me in the arm and tell me I'm wrong!'

It was as dull and intricate as illness. Diamond curlicues, brown roses, vague heraldry. 'How do you receive Feste's work?'

'Well my heart's about to burst so I'll be quick! The fact is I've never met Mr Feste! Every once in a badger moon his manuscripts show up with full rights granted! I can find one if you like! You're not the first to ask! There was a theory that Feste is the Rook or that one inspired the other! Such protracted visions are unhealthy but grand!'

'Do you have a manuscript I can study?'

He ran from the room, kicking through finch tickets and conquest maps in primary colours. Nightjar picked up an unbound rag from the floor. *The Venomist Manifesto*. And here was a piece of *Doctor Clock's Journal*. Surgeons spoke of those ghoulish cases when a heart has a sort of face. Clock looked inside a man's head expecting to see the complications of a watch and found the confusions of climate.

The demented merchant re-entered with a scruffy sheaf of pages. 'Here's the latest, *Truth's Flying Visit* – sadly the last thing I shall ever publish! So few real book eaters it's not worth the candle! The marks on it are typographical, not clues! I would say he was a survivor of the education system, wouldn't you? And the very package it came in! Are you sure I can't interest you in a daisychain design?'

Varnished in sweat, he had a seemingly sarcastic seizure while maintaining eye contact throughout, a smile on his face. He gave off the sickly radiance of a preserved saint that had gone over. She read a few lines. 'Decisions disintegrate by the million, ploughed under.' And 'plough' spelled the Albion way. 'Blindborn laws worse than any villain.' The shape of it was taking its limpid place in the tidepool detail of her mind. She was hypnotized and appalled by the weave of the thing. Only one working without any of the setbacks and diversions of peer approval could pour such flavours into the brain. He just blazed past without consulting anyone. It was only secondarily a book. It suspended the reader in gemlike geometries, an electric urgency like treasure. The envelope was hand-written and the manuscript typed by machine, but not Jonah Robeck's.

'We're going to be good friends, detective, you and me!'

'In actual fact, you give me the creeps, and you may be suffering from ink fever. Would it surprise you to know I entered this discussion with a reasonable belief that you were a sane man? From your expression I see you have little intention of ever being so. This entire place is intolerable.'

There was a squawk from a speaking tube but the man ignored it. 'Our nose and ears keep growing in the grave, remember! And beetles by the hour! A body honoured among bugs! Books are just a bit of pretending! They're not even dependable anymore, professor – did you see? The text on printed books won't sit still! I had a look at *War and Peace* the other day and it was all about a time the wind changed direction and a second horizon briefly appeared with a smattering of surprised-looking puppeteers in evidence, massive as you please! But it doesn't matter to most people and they just carry on!'

'That isn't possible,' she said dismissively, still studying the bundle of papers.

'Oh books are at the mercy of the tides, mother! What I learnt in thirty years of the publishing trade – repetition is a winner! Repeated flowers, arches, ducks, swans, merry and meaningless on a wall! My emporium of recurrence! A sort of purgatory in which I begin to run mad, yes! I've always been an enterprising fellow – and drastic! Last week I removed my trousers unchallenged and realised nobody really knows anything! Since then I've been eating ice cream for its own sake and other dreadful bargains! Well, you can see for yourself! I used to think there was something unethical about screaming out loud! Now I'm the best there is! Unprocessed anger dictates that I nimbly evade the facts! Watch me dodge! I spring, I spring! I tried unrepeating wallpaper and nobody wanted it! Then I had a brainwave! History is scenic trouble! History generates a pattern which is repetitive enough to use as decoration we can all ignore – look here! It's like one plus one over and over, equalling one! I told it to my own reflection in a puddle near the fish market and found the idea very reasonable!

Found the idea very reasonable! Found the idea very reasonable!'

It was a series of bruises repeated thousands of times like medieval arches.

'Here's my latest, tested on the best – targets on a gold field! A fib from my private reserve! Persian wallpaper, selling a dream! Cheap transcendence! Exhaustion in Cairo and exotic cigarette! Say what you must to sell your wares! Gumption alone holds our bones together, if tailors are to be believed! I'll live off jam and fantasy till the profits knock! And when I make my fortune, it's curtains! Curtains!'

He began bucking wildly, drool flashing out of his mouth.

In the Raven Method there was a thing called a convergence point. Nightjar had spent a lifetime assessing the proximity of one stupidity to another, chaos to chaos. Crossed wires sometimes – not often – chanced upon truth. Looking at the wallpaper, Nightjar saw a connection as direct as the articulation of a joint. It was a gas-lamp moment.

As she left that terrible place, the man had put on a Saracen helmet and was jouncing in place with the oar in his hands, screaming about his 'pull-out section'. This we shall pass over in silence, like a goose who can't be bothered.

§

Tom was setting about the finest debacle since the farcical dismount of his birth. He entered his rooms in Shroomsbury, struggling to shuffle off a parsley-coloured 'town swell' frock coat and a striped waistcoat with indigo stars, beneath which was a postman's uniform and three pairs of trousers. Running a hand through his mess of mustard-coloured hair, he knocked the sloped topper to the floor along with a beard like a stack of scallop shells. He was laughing so hard at his own exploits, he took a moment to notice the presence which hulked black as a tar-barrel in his parlour. Inspector Nightjar was standing next to the divan, aiming an oily service pistol at his head. Daylight in cross-section. She had caught him midway between Percy Valentine and two other personas. The surprise bumped him into a momentary blankness.

'I'm caught,' he said, with a gasp of laughter. 'And my false nose is melting like a candle, do you see?'

'It seems you've let your wardrobe get the better of you. And you could use a haircut or two.'

'In fact I was hoping to see your rock-salt hairstyle again. In expectation, I brought a balloon.' He produced the blunt Benko revolver and levelled it.

'Hard to be coiled and passive at the same time but you manage it.'

'What gave me away?'

'Wallpaper.'

'Wallpaper?' To Tom, inadvertence was a kind of magic, an honest-to-god dynamo blade that spun off sideways into a dollhouse if you were lucky. Wallpaper? 'I suppose you'll want me to confirm something.'

'The most common arrangement is a rearguard plea for mercy.'

A dare was a baffling summons without reward or authority, but this? Her disapproval required such a reduction in understanding it was very like being condemned by a flounder. 'After that?'

'You'll be executed in appreciation of your crimes.'

'I'm familiar with validation. I mean to her.'

She frowned. Perhaps she hadn't a clue after all.

'Don't look so puzzled, Inspector,' he said carefully, eying the exits. 'You might give yourself away, like laughing too hard at a slaughterhouse. You're on the trail of ceiling cracks when the building itself stands condemned.'

'If you mean Sophie, she may escape sentence. Pull the trigger. At that point I will be powerless to help you.'

'You don't need to tell me how powerless you

are,' Tom said, moving incrementally. 'You're stuck onto nothing.'

'And who do you think they'll believe – you or the police?'

'A stone unheld's as heavy.'

'Paradox is a cheap gimmick.'

'Yes, coloured glass really.'

'I like coloured glass.'

'So do I.'

Tom blasted a hole through her galvanised hair and the entire barnet burst into flames. As he bolted, she slapped at her hair with one hand and discharged her pistol, hitting the giant copper gong with a spang of portent. Tom slammed through the real exit between the facades at the rear.

Climbing onto the roof and running to the peak of an awning, Tom looked back to see Nightjar emerging from the ladder chute, her head smouldering like a cigar. 'It's my birthday!' he called. 'Let's do something really dangerous!'

It was not his birthday. But as he ran across the tilted rooftops, a ragged figure hobbled by half-off jackets and layered trousers, he felt an exultation. He knew well the second city which hung from ropes and cables between the towers. It was an easy blur of suspended cabins, scabbed minarets and high-tension cables. He crossed gangways and wobbling rope ladders, sliding down steeples and batting through sailcloth. He glanced back. Chugging like a train, Nightjar was ducking under washing lines and slapping at dangled ravellings of hemp and telegraph wire. She thundered over a panel of painted rust. Tom could see the Fairfax Tower behind her.

Vaulting toward a battered door and grabbing for the handle, which was in fact a large snail, Tom hit the door face-first. It was swollen shut. His false nose and the real one were pulped together and the sky was fizzing as he stumbled on. A stepped roof, and a single thin spar linking across to the Skydome. He jangled across this like a puppet and landed on the huge glass bubble, moving forward. Squares of glass were falling out of the curved roof as Tom trudged across it.

This headache was a masterpiece. Checkerfields in the upper head. Non-existent zigzags frazzling in his face. He saw it laid sizzling like a griddle over the city. Albion going stale as it inherited in circles. What else to do?

He turned and raised the revolver at Nightjar, who was landing unsteadily at the rim of the dome. She crouched a moment and then stood to get her bearings. Tom fired at her, hitting nothing. When he saw her outline devolving repeatedly within her form it occurred to him she was her own person.

If this is death I'm the man for it, he thought, dizzy with everything. *I've had it with oxygen*. He thought of Sophie and her bombshell dreams. The striated glass was snapping and crunching under his boots like river ice. And the sky for moral support. The Benko went off in his hand, blowing space out from under him.

§

Tom dropped fifty feet, fast in splashing glass. He crimped a connecting strut on the way down and spun like a starfish, then smacked to the floor of the tea court. The little orchestra stopped playing.

One grandee peered over his collar with the curiosity of a hot air balloonist. Some ne'er-do-well had shockingly exposed his bones in public. Laying in a bundle, he was a crafty one, this patchwork fellow with the bleeding hair and yolk hanging out of his eyes. He sported a yellow silk cravat and what appeared to be a lung, pink as a doll. A potted plant had toppled over. There was quite a fuss, and several complaints.

16

Bombazine

In an office high in the Towers of Parliament, Nightjar gave a briefing to the Chancellor of the Circuit, using her field notes. The anarchist connection had brought her to the Chancellor's attention, though he wished to see it a very particular way. Roger Swive was a man in whom stupidity had been perfected and made, by his authority, inescapable for everyone else. He had never had an accurate moment in his life and decreed something one minute which he couldn't recall the next. On a good day he could be depended upon to take the right idea in the wrong direction. His veined bulge of a head had scared his hair away and he had compensated by growing a moustache like a tobacco moth.

The wood and stone office was so cunningly carven, so chambered in darkly recessed detail, that Nightjar felt like a bug lodged in a cadaver. She supposed that in such a reduced scenario you must eat the walls. Ignoring her discomfort, she stated the facts with a measured clarity – continuing even when Swive boggled or yelped – until the account was complete. Swive then asked her to repeat the matter he had missed when boggling and yelping.

Valentine's rooms had proved a bonanza of evidence. He had acquired much of his aesthete garb at a boutique called Shirt Perilous, popular with mollies and theatre folk. Where the Inspector's shot had dented the gong it later came apart in two halves like a shell, leaking a galore of incrimination. Forged permits, ballistic talismans, a block of Rook calling cards, reports of his transgressions pressed in a keepsake album, and one of the plates for the banknotes which had dented trust in the Albion pound for several days. And a letter in vermillion ink:

Darling Dynamite,

We did a lot to love within this tiger's maw. Binaries make a meal of us. When two people disagree, they curate a space between them for reality to take place. Some call it the Conception of Fools, but ours was a clean crash. You struck me as a polychrome blaze and I

can never see you any other way. I only want to go
where you go. For someone like me, it's shameful. But
none of us get through without scars. I am blotted by
the intensity of your heaven-born disasters. We'll kiss
as everything explodes upward around us. I love you.

War Girl

'Here's a file containing everything,' she
concluded.

'Creamy and tantalizing,' said Swive, taking it.
'I'm gratified at your relentless pursuit of agitators,
abnormals, dissidents, militants, malcontents,
radicals, remonstrants and bargain-hunters here in
the capital.'

'And not a few criminals,' Nightjar suggested
tersely.

'It's well-known you've solved several acclaimed
murders. You support me and my constant work
– that work against revolutionaries and defiance
clusters who fill my every waking hour with their
interminable chat. It's been a busy few days, for us
and the Rook. Talion, dead – the man who kept
the lights on! Murder is offputting isn't it?'

'I doubt the Rook had anything to do with it.'

'When the nurse found Talion's body – an hour
after you left his side, Inspector – there was a Rook

calling card in his clawlike hand. It seems he evaded you with ease.'

'I'm not sure of the timeframe, and the design of that card was reproduced in every newspaper. Anyone could make one.'

'Garinati, Ossipon, Gregory, Pinelli, Hartmann? They're idiots. We hope for at least the semblance of a motive but these buggers aren't even on the make.'

'You assume the villain is from a known chapter. I can suspect a thousand people at a time.'

'Good show. Blame anyone at all costs.'

'That isn't quite what I mean. Most revolutionaries can be safely spayed by placing them before an audience. People follow any luminous oaf who entertains them. The theatre is quite openly called a diversion. Let's accept the clue. The man I chased down, Valentine or Owen or whatever he called himself, was a showman. Talion's killer inspires no-one and simply does it all himself.'

'Do you have sympathy with any of these radicals?'

'Truth is seen as a sacred difficulty. I'm in accord with that.'

'Truth speaks with a small face like a candleflame. Too much passion and you blow it out. Admix a clear outlook with a diseased fancy, you find yourself with an inflammatory mutualism – and hens walking in daylight down the boulevard!'

'We already have such hens, Chancellor. They strut in the muddy streets and their feathers are bleak.'

'The "patterns" which led you to Valentine – are these real patterns or just faces in the fire?'

She was affronted that he of all people was accusing her of acting without reference to reality. 'I was suspicious because none of his ideas looked like themselves, inside. The articles among the dead man's effects prove I was right.'

'Happenstance but nevertheless extraordinary. Charred your famous hair, I see! Followed by the underhand excursion you describe and a show-stopping fall through the skylight! What did he hope to gain by having legs like that? And nine pairs of trousers!'

'It was three pairs, merely. Layers of disguise.'

'Valentine was known to wear outlandish attire. I met him once. His arms had twenty-five sleeves. Each. And you may be sure he drew attention to them with unnecessary gestures as he annoyed everyone with some dismal lampoon. Waving something he called a "johnny stick". I had to crane my neck to make sure he saw my disapproval.'

'The important point is, this man was the Rook.

A set of Rook cards were found in his rooms.'

'But you say yourself, anyone can print them. And this other fellow, a shopkeeper of nervous and neurotic aspect, seems as effective as a glass hammer.'

Nightjar thought about that unassuming fellow and broadly agreed with the Chancellor's estimation. She had a man watching the shop in Drood Street and Jonah Robeck had not returned. 'Did you investigate a link between the Rook and the author Emmanuel Feste?'

He looked thoughtful. 'At some time, I believe. It came to nothing.'

'The package in which his latest screed was delivered bore the same handwriting as this letter. And both match specimens of Sophie's hand provided by Lord Shafto.'

'Well as to the letter it looks like a fanatical blandishment to the poet Valentine. The link between Feste and the Rook is unproven, and I doubt it. The average scribe's hollowed out by the urge to instruct others and by the end he's spent, the fever past you might say. While in his mind, he's smashed the world with justice. But Feste or not, figures like the Rook are rather useful.'

'He's hardly the undisputed dean of mayhem.

Those banknotes replacing "sum" with "bum" were basically childish.'

'But when distributed they did sow economic doubt didn't they? His renegade magnanimity wobbled our finances for a fortnight. What matters is his compelling reputation as an outlaw behind a barleycorn mask, distracting with some second-rate outrage while operationally not being too much of a menace. As far as the common people know, the Rook can be angry about five things at once and pitches a bomb into an office at the drop of a hat. He wasn't born, he was broken off into this world like the end of a bottle! That image of him may be no more real than a waiter's reassurance but people are confounded by the easiest lie. Put a crab in a bargain's location and they clamour for the crab.'

This much was true, but she and the Chancellor seemed to be skirting so far around the real subject that their orbit was barely maintained. Trying to navigate such changeable constructions was giving her a cramp in the head. She squeezed her eyes together in a try for clarity. 'Sophie Shafto is missing. That is the complaint I have been asked to address.'

'Yes, a terrible business. I'm up to my lips in Shafto rail shares myself.'

'If you are maintaining that the Rook is

behind Sophie's abduction, we do indeed have a demonstrable link between the Rook and Feste. The ransom note quotes directly from the passage on page twenty-three of this vitriolic pamphlet against evil.'

She slapped *Truth's Flying Visit* onto the desk before him. As he scrutinised it, she gazed at the wall of desiccated accolades behind him. 'Potboiler is it?' said Swive at last, bewildered but amiable. 'I'm used to being disparaged behind my shoulders, old girl. I can take a joke!'

Nightjar snatched the book up and looked at the page where the 'war's manifold misdirection' passage appeared. She found instead something about 'flesh and reluctance'. It seemed to be a theory of colour corrosion applied to morality and the development of acid-flake excuses whose intensity sizzled the mind.

Nightjar was stunned. It was such an unexpected problem, like a squirrel that doesn't get out of the way.

Swive steepled his hands and leaned forward. 'Miss Nightjar. Beatrix – may I call you that?' he decided, smiling slimily. 'Beatrix, we are both charged with prettifying the internal security of the state. It never ends – like cleaning a mackerel. But the Raven Method has long been in doubt.

Reality seen seven ways like a smashed sandwich! Meanwhile there are real dangers out there. Do you know there's a bear running loose in town? Bold as brass! Clowns are on the increase, and I intend to propose "gallivanting" as an offence, as "acting well amid a fray" could mean several things. And there's been a colourful spate of poetic outbursts on the Machine Mile. To work with cities – what reward? At least rain reminds me it's not all my decision.'

'Chancellor Swive,' the Inspector announced in an attempt to draw a line under his gibberish. 'You seem determined to curtail my investigation. I tell you I have killed the Rook and you want to keep him publicly on the boil.'

'A discredited activist is a sad thing. You have killed a bad poet and probable mandrake. An epicure in the pinched instant of the exquisite – that's the time to clobber him! An orientalist is out of his own hair at last. And now, all the real razzle-dazzle of disintegration! No, that plodding partisan the Rook is still at large and six moves ahead of us. Bad moves, thankfully.'

'Well,' Nightjar swallowed. 'As it happens you may be partly right. The Rook could in fact be two people. I believe the other to be Sophie Shafto, who still lives.'

Swive was aghast. 'What possible evidence could

you have for some Darjeeling completist to have done... well, anything at all?'

'Her handwriting on the envelope in which the manuscript of this tract was delivered.'

'If Sophie Shafto has become confused and taken up with an amateur hothead murmuring muddle-headed notions of agrarian joy or some other idea from the back of beyond, all the more reason to bring her to safety and set her straight!' He rapped decisively on the desktop.

Clarity, she thought as she left the hideous building and breathed deep in the night air. *Barrelling out of chaos, you'll never get it.* She consoled herself with the thought that Swive would be devoured by his own importance until he was a fish-comb in a drain. She had presented her proofs and he had taken the trouble to ignore each one individually. For Nightjar the only surprise in Valentine's parlour was the letter, belying as it did Sophie's infamous composure. But a full-tilt human being didn't have that symmetry which allowed an accurate prediction of the sides which were out of view.

§

Two miles away, Sophie brought Tom's Sparks Landau within aiming distance of Caledonia Tower. At the vehicle's rear: two giant wheels like penny farthings on either side of a large glass globe in which tendrils of plasmic energy clawed at the inner surface. At the front: an exposed assembly of valves like a cathedral and two small central wheels. In the centre: the plush love seat where Sophie was lowering the roof canopy and tying off the guiding rod. She stepped out of the car and assured herself of an accurate slant across the darkened street. She wore a gown of bombazine and black satin, with antlered shoulders in imitation of the frondy collar of an axolotl. With the Landau's howling static charge, her hair stood up like the spines of an urchin.

Caledonia was a tower of hoops, each storey looking roughly the same since it was painted over dark blue. When Sophie leaned into the Landau to release the brake, the vehicle accelerated fast. It baulked over a kerb and ploughed into the ground floor, its snout crumpling and the rear exploding under the building. The ribs of three upper floors thudded downward, blasting smoke into the road. She felt the heat instantly dry her tears as the street was illuminated.

17

Subtraction

Nightjar walked along a metal gantry which skirted the main turbine hall of the Brewster Dodgeworks. The chamber was strangely airless and echoed with repetitive noise. She found Jay Brewster spectating his workers from the railing ahead, his hair the colour of wet rust. Apart from a pair of safety goggles he was dolled up as though attending a cocktail party. He seemed unfazed by her approach and called out. 'You're late coming to see me Inspector. Aren't I the most likely culprit in the dastardly abduction of Sophie Shafto?' He removed his goggles and handed them to her. 'Best wear these goggles against the reversal atmospherics or you might see the opposite of what you're told. We have a pressure leak, I don't know where it's going and it's getting worse. Those engineers you see there are checking everything.' He called down. 'Nobby! Check the gaskets! Nobby's the one in the stupid overalls and futuristic hat. A rubber sombrero, I like it.' He yelled down again and pointed at his own head. 'I like it, Nobby! We're always making refinements, Inspector. Themes and schemes. Now, you're here about the Shafto girl. I'm acquainted with her and I don't know if she's tough or screwball. Maybe both – the deluded often get things done.'

Nightjar pulled the goggles over her eyes and the rarefied air became visible as a kind of colourless, scrambling absence. She felt suddenly empty. 'It's true an idiot sometimes expedites right action, but you don't strike me as the kind to live by chance.'

'Really? Law's a blade big enough to flick a man in half. And law is beholden to chance – you know it, Inspector. Is she sane enough to be hanged, I wonder? In any case I'd be amazed if she's been abducted at all.'

'What makes you say that?'

'Sophie has radical political beliefs and is perfectly capable of faking her own disappearance, with her father's help probably. Tell her an objection and she just up and considers it carefully.'

'Why would he help her?'

'He knows his army bid is sub-par and needs an excuse to withdraw and save face. His project's nothing more than an oversize gas pistol. Fires billiard balls with his eyes and nose lightly embossed on the surface. Talion's cannon works on electrified gas that goes jagged like lightning, impossible to aim. My vacuum gun on the other hand is fully in line with military objectives. Negates the very existence of the enemy as a sentient force, and simply subtracts them – rather like sweeping away the dry flakes of an old onion and leaving the room with a smirk. That's a winner. There's a real art to weapons. Be careful you don't give a predator such big teeth it can't eat.'

Nightjar was trying to adapt to the fluttering vacuum which permeated everything. Brewster himself seemed eaten down by its toxicity – his body looked like a cored husk. 'Yes, I have interviewed your industrial associates from the Donimo.'

'And they all say it's hokum, right?' Brewster grinned, emptiness howling around him. 'Can't run a car on snake oil, ma'am – my stuff's for real.'

'You heard about Talion's death?'

'Even signed a paper to say it surprised me. Hell of a thing. Talion taught us how to shiver with fright at our firesides, the old crank. Head like the back of a flower. Hid wings in his mouth like a bug. Creepy as a child and what was he, ninety-seven? That's the age to be. Not a skeleton yet but just as scary. And able to say opinions, ghoulish opinions.

And not give a damn because, hey I'm nearly a skeleton, okay? This time next year. Anyway I'll miss him.'

'Yours was a compact of convenience?'

'There was such an equilibrium of reproach between us I daresay we were very like friends. Same with Shafto and his great cannonball of a head. He sits in his tin citadel and does no harm. Thinks he's got a raw deal because the world moved on. A titan of steam ain't much these days.'

'You don't like him.'

'I like the side I can see. We're both self-assembled and we rarely quarrel above a whisper. I believe his face has learned lessons and it hasn't gone deeper than that. But I like that about him, the off-the-rails buffer and his outdated eyebrows. How did poor old Valentine describe him? "bloviating pomposity".'

'Valentine said you were prodding "fraudulent furnaces".'

'I'll make you a deal, Inspector. Let me show you around the station. I offer safe conduct across my explanation. I'm not betting everything on bunk. There's a real mechanism at work. And if you're not convinced by the end I'll shred my britches.'

She followed him around the station, ducking under pipes and peering at gauges as Brewster explained it all, sometimes shouting above the clamour.

'Take a look at these ordeal cylinders fitted with diachronic-suppressive valves. Solid state, you could say. Those things that look like pumps are actually just sitting there. In fact this main cognition hall basically radiates itself, a sort of aching staleness. The mounting tension avoids these junctions and transpires through pipework to the ramification plate, which stops it dead – basically a hermetic battery. I wish it glowed like a firefly jar but gadzooks it sure is sickly, look at that! These endlessly convulving hammer gears don't connect with anything. This is why observers have insisted my device is all legerdemain, but this sort of contentless repetition is crucial, I assure you. Relays.' He pointed to a silo below a ring of painted wooden magnets. 'This is a parallax vat, denial so stale and baked-in it stinks to high heaven, though we don't notice. The vat is vacuum-sealed but only because no air can be admitted. At first I used ceramic vessels to avoid false conduction, but later realised nobody cared. Pat satisfaction with paradox is a deflection. What are the gears and levers within it, and why do we like it so much that we leave it alone? In this case the vat has a girdle of anti-culminating rods, and those colophon valves are all inhibitors, nearly a thousand of them arrayed throughout the facility. Everything else is outside.'

'What are these vacuum tubes for? Sending information?'

'No ma'am,' Brewster chuckled, and did not elaborate.

In this strangely eventless apparatus, nothing felt transactional and there was a grey malignance that made her watchful. How could something so unhealthy be so clean? 'Are those bilge tanks?'

'No ma'am, there is no run-off. Maybe that's a clue. What do you see?'

She did not mention the patterns of stagnation pinning every object to itself. 'What I see is a mill full of unimaginative devices apparently invented for spite.'

'No, for cash. Though one can soak up the other.'

They made their way to the prospect chamber which overlooked the main hall, where they sat at a broad glass desk. Nightjar took off her goggles. She had a poison headache. On the wall hung a map of the Ricochet Wars, a portrait of Howell Cobb already swollen with the pride which would kill him, and a photogram of PT Barnum kicking a horse.

Brewster was pleased with himself. 'So you see? People assume it's an act of impoverishment resulting in toxic rarefication, but it's more like the busy compression that results from fierce denial. That compression is a battery. A productive incoherence. It's the movement of energy according to scientific law. A thing must be a certain way because any other possibility would be unbearable or unacceptable. When I was a kid working in my dad's feed store a Dutch potato farmer introduced me to Swedenborg and the Cloudists. Before that I was following the comic antics of Irrigation Alligator and Calarity the Cat. Now I read everything I could. I dabbled in what the boffins were calling the ether, a dumping ground for all we evade. Well as your friends in the north say, "Where there's muck there's brass." But it became perfectly clear to me that it was the very working of denial – evasion, self-deception, fear – that entailed the greatest movement of energy. And that could be haltered and used for the many pastimes that consume us in the modern day. It was a discovery concealed by its own nature, Inspector – I was pragmatic enough to look it straight in the eye.'

'And what did you see, Mr Brewster?' Nightjar asked, with enough languor to suggest that she didn't care.

'Something strange. But in hindsight, rather obvious. A great tangle of used stuff, all angles, all true, and somehow in a perpetual state of un-knitting. And at the same time, a celestial suspension of somehow intervolving creative nectar.'

'Now you begin to sound like Valentine.'

Brewster waved dismissively. 'I put my knowledge to use. I don't know what he did. You'd think a particle's pinhole abyss would be horrible. What surprised me, about my "vision" I mean, was how rich it all is, even the dirt – all of it is treasure. And that stood absolutely to reason.'

'I would expect the mass of denied truth to be thoroughly toxic.'

'Oh no, ma'am – we're the ones who denied it. The toxins stay right here with us, dripping off the walls.' He gestured expansively, smiling.

'This explains the ambivalence we all feel on an evasion-propelled locomotive.'

'The notion that an honest man aboard interferes with the engine? That shows a lack of engineering knowledge.'

'Nevertheless every slowing-down or stop in the middle of nowhere has us looking askance at our fellow passengers, wondering who's the innocent.'

'Instead of pretending it isn't happening, as they should.'

'You admit their influence is relevant?'

'They can make no difference, as I think you know. But it's their duty to pretend all is well. When they venerate a vacuum it makes my job easier. The principle whereby a thing which wants to move is forced to be inert. The energy in that inertia. It's propulsive, for those who would use it. You and I both profit from that holding-in-place so that a label may be assigned and the thing itself dies. The intricate resistances of a gear system are a hassle, and then the wasteful release. There's a finite profit in that sort of thing. A lot more in a sort of airless smothering. Did you ever strangle a chicken, Inspector? You can adjust the octave of its cries by twisting the neck. I remember one of my early experiments at the O'Leary's in Chicago. I kept the pressure on a force that struggled all the more to live. It amazed me. Then I fetched up here – Thousand Tower City! A stuck-up town of redoubts and keeping rooms, all enhaloed with surmise. A heartboggling foolscape extending in all directions. Hallelujah. Nothing doing, resolutely, until the old spiked fiend is strangled by its own black railings. For centuries it's been sinking into itself and we're all taking bets on the bottom. Every one of the thousand towers is made to dwarf human scale. To live in, let's say, a cosy cottage or some such, we might get ideas of our own. Architecture is a blood sport. People here are satisfied with guesses and running on fumes. The human brain comprises almost three pounds of evasion and excuses. The less of them lay claim to their own minds the better – but that's true of so many things isn't it? The trick is keeping them alive while not thinking. Human endurance. And we're doing rather well here in the capital. You see, if a chaos is particulated enough, you can direct it like a liquid. Or at best, freeze it into batteries so that fear is artificially perennial. If we must have seasons, make them short and random. You don't want people using them as metaphors or a means of perspective.'

Nightjar realised she was exhausted, as if the strength had been sucked from her cells. 'Is all of this true?'

'If you catch it at the right moment.'

'No, then. Do me the service of lying more convincingly. Does no-one care anymore?'

'You're wound a little tight yourself, Inspector. I like it. Shrewd and diligent, fastidious, tenacious – rare qualities in these underpowered times. The law's come so far it looks like a thing from another world. I hear an ungrateful member of the public paid a visit to Caledonia Tower. Any leads?'

'They used Percy Valentine's car, so it may

have been one of his acolytes. Witnesses say the perpetrator dressed in his style.'

'Flamboyant even when in a hurry, am I right? I liked Valentine's incantations but you'd get better sense stamping on a can.'

'Either way, an explosion resolves itself rather quickly.'

'You're right, the real action is elsewhere. The perfect crime is to swallow someone whole. For that you need a community. Or a whale. They say hell is full of fire, people and incoherence.'

Nightjar thought of the intense and contentless void she had seen through the goggles. 'Some say it's all that but very cold.'

'That would make it like any city in the nation, wouldn't it?' he laughed. He was playing absently with a pyramidal dice from the Orient. 'Are you any closer to finding Sophie Shafto?'

'One hindrance to the deductive method is incomplete information – if more than one of these gaps is plugged with conjecture, the whole thing becomes a fantasy.'

'Sounds delicious. The gulf between your aims and mine is frankly staggering in its own right. We ought to bottle and market the thing. Better still, equate a thing with an unlike quality and you set off a cascade pattern of misunderstanding. Look what they've done with the word "anarchism", defined as its opposite. That's genius right there.'

'Something of the kind has been happening to books,' Nightjar told him. 'But not the incoherence you adore. Definitions stay the same. New narratives. It's rather lush.'

'What do you mean?'

'Published books are becoming filled with new ideas. Like a flood of creativity while everyone is looking elsewhere.'

'Is that so?' he said, with real interest. Nightjar felt she was seeing the edge of some private emotion. 'Is that so.'

'Yes. After all, nobody's reading them, and when the cat's away. I discovered it in connection with Sophie. Remember the ransom note?' She handed *Truth's Flying Visit* across the desk. 'Look at page twenty-three, the middle passage, and tell me what you see.'

'Did Sophie write this?' he asked, taking it, and Nightjar realised, in a private surprise that felt like a flower, *Yes, of course she did.* Almost at once the sap flowed back into her body. Sophie's symphonic awareness was like the dripping workface of a honey mine.

Brewster read from the page, frowning. '"Never a brave man, god turned nasty"' he began, baffled, and more which burst riches of red gold brainfruit into the air around him. The book had changed again within a few days.

'I have to go,' Nightjar said quietly, wading out through juice and treasure.

§

After Inspector Nightjar had left, walking as if she was wading through something, former Lieutenant Frank Lukas entered by the side door. Brewster was amused to see that he was wearing the pink and chocolate uniform he had been issued. 'Well look who's finally awake despite the safeguards. Middleman! Did you hear much of that?'

'What you just said to me?' Lukas asked, drinking prodigiously from a leather flask and slurping his nose. It had transpired that he had a bull's tongue where others have a brain and could only think when his mouth was open. He was cupshot most of the time and for a little longer would be fun to befuddle.

'You're a real turn-up for the books, Middleman. Listen to this lie while it's still fresh in my mind. I've always wondered, why is it considered safe to be in the world with a fellow whose want is equal to mine? When we have, as the poet said, all the permanence of pastry? Ah, poets will even fill the sky with words. But you and I know, a cluster of symmetries may pose for a system of the world, but the world itself won't know it and carries on regardless.'

'Always on the lookout for sense, me.' Lukas blinked at him.

'You look baffled as a dog in a plum enclosure. Didn't you just hear me say that what appears to be lack of courage may in fact be an excess of wonder? I know patriotism is more than the lustre it gives to horror, but you're on the way up, champ! Anyone with a vestful of meat and a hatful of head can join the army. Take an oath and pretty soon you're boiling your belt, right? And collecting wounds like rare wines, alongside other armed acrobats. I saw an admiral once. He was spattered with medals like bits of egg. It was nothing to the living medals on a reptile. That uniform of yours, rocking boy, speaks so eloquently of your fear, why raise a weapon? You'll suspect a fellow's weak if he wears a helmet won't you? What happens when you cut in half a thing that's the same all the way through?'

'Reduce the amount and that's all,' said Lukas thickly.

'Very good. I like your confidence, Middleman. You're going to see that nearly everyone can be a supplicant, of one sort or another. That's the core and glory of it. People think MPs are mere drones but you know they have personal volition when you have to bribe them individually.'

'What are you talking about.'

'There is a man,' Brewster declared, playing with the book on his desk, 'whose stupidity is a matter of public record. Chancellor Roger Buridan Swive. A brain the consistency of banana, a stickleback on his coat of arms and a face which cries out for your fist and mine. Thinks he inaugurates every room he enters. He can tell lies all day without repeating himself. Wears masks on his knees. Believes he'll enter heaven with a mouthful of lamb. With as few extraneous principles as possible, he's forthright but not exceptional. Loud without content. In summary, he's my kind of man – a double-headed man! One is his own, very small, and the other stuffed with luggage – family, profession, and diplomacy. I'm going to go bang those heads together. A real evangelist only sees in one direction. We can use that, the way a folded sheet of paper will also fold the other way along the same line.'

'Politics isn't my strong suit, sir. Uncanny terrain.'

Brewster studied the beleaguered tower on the cover of *Truth's Flying Visit*. 'Those dried rodents in Parliament rattle the same dead as alive. No leaks there. Even you've got more juice.' He stood to look through the observation window at the power floor. 'Break machinery apart to its smallest bit and you won't find evil, soldier.'

'What then.'

'Emptiness, sport. Emptiness set running. Well maybe that is evil, after all. You've emptied yourself out at the behest of anyone who'd fill you with repetition, the infernal machinery. But to my investors thankfully I walk on plain water. See how I trust you? You're no dummy, slugger. No, you're not.'

§

Nightjar's notes: Jay Brewster, an Amerikaan who dismisses anything pre-dating his buttocks. A surface flush with personality, he lies all over himself. At best I'd describe his reasoning as 'tantalizing'. He has the skill of affability. He looks real in my right eye and not in my left. His excuses lead off in every direction, their architecture beyond me. To what extent does he believe his own assertions, or keep track of them? I modified his central argument twenty-seven times and never got a viable construct. It's like the story of the cobbler who bought an idea at market, and by the time he'd got it home and unknotted it there was nothing left. And to save his shame he convinced himself that the idea had been in the structure. There's more substance in

*a whisked ghost than in this charmer. And to think
that I believed Valentine an exponent of nothing but
himself! We expect evil to be snorting like a stove, but
it's chill as vinegar.*

18

A Fond Reunion

Sophie's father looked out on a quiet, magnetic horizon. He seemed almost to be posing on the high brass terrace as Sophie stepped out onto its old familiar grooves and patterns. 'Look at that, Quadfrey,' he said, not looking back. 'A sky of insurmountable light. Some irregularities in the clouds perhaps. The weather's doubting itself.'

'It's me, father,' she announced, and he turned, startled. 'I took it for granted you would hate me and here I am.'

Shafto twitched as though a dozen different plans had suggested themselves in an instant, his eyes darting about. Sophie was in her street urchin gear and looked slightly more forsaken than she was. With a glance down at the ornamented chess yard, Lord Shafto settled into some sort of resolve. 'Was it that infantryman?'

'What are you talking about?'

'You threw yourself at this disaster like a lovesick drunk. Betrayal in the raw. And now you dare toddle in here dirty as a doll in a trunkful of rocks? Hang your legs in shame! Is it the Clowning Sickness? A nostalgia for the Vivid Age and its lurid nonsense? Some memories are allowed to get so fat with feeding, I swear they demand more than the present! Where have you been sleeping?'

'Near the river. Rashes and snot are my constant companions.'

'When you've rooms in Helgravia, full of your favourite gowns? Who was it?'

'If it must be anyone, I suppose you knew him as Percy Valentine.'

'That unlamented jackaroon? I heard you sent a letter of hearts and kisses, but to a man who referred to his own brain as a "skull blossom" and his nose as a "pelmet"? He talked to me about crows once. For three minutes I lived happy in the belief that he was working towards a point. I took it into my monstrous head that he valued my time. And then the realisation, and the anger. The anger! Do you know how you've vexed me, child? What possessed you to do it?'

'I possess myself. One can only revolutionise oneself, with any certainty.'

'And by reading Feste, I suppose. That's right,

I've informed myself thoroughly on your recent fodder.'

Sophie felt miserable. 'I so do not want to keep secrets from you, father. You force the necessity upon me. But here I am, and precious little else. A skull and other sundries.'

'A fine anguish!' A thin snow had begun percolating over the Steel Tower. 'While I'm up to my cheeks in infamies. A complete punishment is beyond the scope of these stubby arms. Even the sky frowns at you – look! Let's get inside.'

'These weather variations are caused by Jay Brewster's denial mills.'

'What otherworldly loon told you that? I daresay you've been feeding at Prospero's – yes, I know about it.' He followed her into the state room where the chrome table was littered with newspapers. 'I've been making discreet inquiries of my own. Privately I cried havoc at considerable expense and you have been seen at Carroll's Hats, Pinglott's, Syme's, Shirt Perilous, Debacle Caps & Costumiers, and in Very Street dressed as a bloody nun! I kept it out of the papers for a week but here it is now – *The Towers Gazette*, *The Thousand Times*, *The Chiliad* – "Headstrong Hoyden in Hurly-Burly". There it is! "Missing heiress consorts with *bouquinistes*." People talk of nothing else!'

'Seen temporally, you know this is thin scandal that nourishes no-one. Tidings should interest at least.'

'Tidings be damned! You were always a bold one but your calm in here fairly takes my breath away. Given the seriousness of the case I'd appreciate a response commensurate with my agitation.'

'Should I be hysterical, just to be amenable?'

'Yes!'

'I won't and you should know that. What are these stage tricks, father? Why are you pretending not to know me? Gossip and fancy? I'm incarnate against such stuff.'

Lord Shafto seemed to twist within. 'Do you have any conception of the to-do you've caused? Do you imagine there's a soul in this city that doesn't know you ran off with book-eaters? Your romp with honesty is the worst thing that's ever happened to me. It's an unbridled rigmarole of scandal and scrutiny, and sure enough, it's as much as I can stand. You could wreck everything.'

'And in record time.'

'What in the blazing world is this revolutionary nonsense? Singing intolerably among some scrappy crew? Am I to be told again I'm a collaborator? I've already got Quintilian rhetoric draining out of my gill arches! And what in the ruddy hellfire is

Floutist anarchy?'

'Floutation is a fad. I don't subscribe. The fact is I went stark raving sane out there – enlightened sky-high. My "scrappy crew" repair the world you erode every day. Which we're not paid for, by the way.'

'A mended thing is changed, you'll find. Besides, child, sometimes through entropy a structure will partly collapse into a more effective or interesting configuration! Why not wait for that?'

'Ah, freedom postponed, a flavour we have grown to love! It's easier to pretend that it makes sense and is to our taste.'

'I'm too experienced for such absolute statements. I forget that your unlined forehead is the final stronghold of all good sense. So wilful and straightforward! You annoy because you always get to the point! You do nothing but! Your conversation's like a swarm of hornets! I could blame this latest folly on your book-learning, but a decision like that has to pass through the heart just as our sugar has to pass through Amsterdaam, a town where weeping is an artform and fish are eaten headfirst while alive. Headfirst, while alive!'

'Understandable to bite the head off a fish so easily available, father. They become blasé.'

'"Blasé" now, is it? I never taught you such words!'

'Yes, you did. You taught me everything, and were my hero once upon a time. I remember. We were in a library with a sunny window.'

Her father looked embarrassed. 'Will you sit down, at least?'

'If it becomes necessary,' she said, and then immediately sat down, not looking at him.

'It's been decided that your emotionality is too oblique.'

She looked at him. For a meaty man he was very susceptible to being stared down. 'What does that mean.'

'You are having the wrong feelings. And I daresay the wrong insights. Bedazzled or brain-stricken, it doesn't help that you're shuttling about like a target. We'll get to the root of your temper, you'll see. I have come to an accommodation with Doctor Sodgery. Already drawn up the papers. Retreat by night has the element of surprise doesn't it? It'll get you out of this public muddle, but your bought safety has a thin floor my dear.'

'Those most chilling of words, "It's all been arranged." We'll not have that conversation again, father.' The mere prospect bored her. The thing itself might kill her.

'Well how would you describe what you're in for? Do you think you can live in the wild, eating butterflies and bark? A lost thing comes loose from its name. You'll end solitary and mangled, like Valentine! You'll be buried like a brace of grubby curtains!'

'And you'll be buried with your blunders like a pharaoh. Nature's sun puts itself at risk every minute.'

'The sun has resources. Why weren't you ever content to be doll-like, twittery, like your friends? There were plenty of boys biting at the balconies.'

'They tormented me for years with their abject cheer, so vacant and expectant. Would you really have me marry some brutish bravo or simpering void? An advantageous marriage – a foot in the door of the slaughterhouse? Dragged tripes-first into the vestry? The brain I was born with made me the object of scorn and worship. For years the situation baffled me. So I resolved to learn the rules of this horse-drawn nightmare. To ignore contradictions. To faint away whenever called upon to do so. To come bending into a room in pretend modesty. I made use of all such lies and gained nothing of interest. I cleared every twisted hurdle and my hard-won increments went unnoticed. For years I forged my own face minute to minute, as you do now! The average mask crushes like an eggshell, so light and unsatisfying, after years of holding power.

And worse, I was expected to aspire to something several people had done already.'

'No matter how novel a notion, it could be more so, is that the song? There's a bloody limit, child, like the number of folds you can put in a thing.'

'Nothing to stop me adding outward, father. And what of *The Angel Index*, in which every full-stop contained another book, as did every full-stop within those books? Didn't you read that to me once? Such books saved my life. Now you consort with men who stump the future and ignore the underdead. The city is complicit, bequeathing its children a world made of our excuses. Such a disjointed destiny, should it be yearned for? Think of the cool silent stillness at the centre of an ignored stone. Well, I decided to keep it company.'

'Until I was at my wits' end, I know.'

'Which was the true life? So many are forced to live segmented selves. The man you knew as Percy Valentine went into the world as the Rook, and is now smeared across eternity.'

'The Rook! I've heard you extolling his blunders but isn't he the vainglorious jackass who rode a mechanical spider down the Machine Mile?'

'A fine rampage during a high watermark for the form. And it was a termite. And a statement!'

'I'm sure the struggling workers were most

grateful. Is that how you "repair the world"? Oh wondrous conspiracy, like perfumes mixing in a coloured garden! Your raindance calls down cordial on your enemies. It's all your fancy, this pious hope to destroy. To uncage this zoo of grievances upon the town?'

'What you take for peace is exhaustion and captivity. And which is it, father? Am I harmless or a threat? Is your argument that I am doing something wrong or that I go about it inefficiently? Tom was unswerving, even when wrong.'

'He murdered poor old Talion!'

'No, he did not.'

'A disciplined bandit? Sounds like a soldier to me. And where is he now? Castling with the king of the world!'

'Rumi, father? At a time like this? It's hard to be courteous and angry at the same time, but he did it. We were each other's guru like roses on the same bush. It was a truly great time in my life. And you brought in the state police?'

'I didn't know which way to turn. I'll admit that hovering hag Nightjar puts the wind up me.' He glanced about as if expecting the Inspector to appear at any moment. 'So, your man, a death of the old school, I heard. Carried off by god's own gravity. You swore to love to the end I suppose.'

'"Until iron floats."'

'Our gun leviathans are made entirely of iron and float rather well I think you'll find. It's war, after all.'

'It's always war, father. Should I have pretended not to notice? You've been nestled into such incentives for decades. The nation's coffers are brimming with foreign blood. Sanctioned pillagers pose as the retaliation industries. Enslavement and slaughter put down to unremitting coincidence.'

'Those modernised by force are always a little dazed at first.'

'An armour-plated orange may impress aesthetically, but to a hungry man? Every civilization is the temporary standing of a dog, before lying down. We don't apply our values consistently. If a white feather means cowardice, what's the meaning of a fern? You received my note. Or was my choice of words too obscure?'

'Yes it most damnably was! "Freakish grace"?'

'You're so engrossed in your own downfall, father. Do you think I always know what I'm about? Can't you see my heart is broken? Poor Tom, who died with the will to justice still in him. I wish his soul had crossed without cargo.'

'Sophie,' he said, more softly. 'I always turned a blind eye to your escapades because I love you. But you never missed an opportunity to think with method and clarity. How do you think it was for us when at any moment you could have one of your fits of logic? Our bafflement was wasted on you. I berated you and you discarded the content. Fattened by my consternation, you went into the world with that devil-may-care calm of yours.'

'Would you have had me relent unduly? For a while I could only conclude that if I accumulated enough admonishments I would win a fabulous prize.'

'Nobody picks up on such complicated umbrage, girl. These extremes now, only pure necessity could excuse it.'

'Yes. Necessity. When the alternative was to absent myself from the world, in one way or other. The things that are said of me contradict each other and that makes them difficult to engage with. That I'm an object without will and yet full of guilt. That I haven't a brain and that I over-use my brain. That I'm weak and yet will damage civilisation. And most insulting, that there are others' opinions riding on my bones like little imps. But my bones are my own and I keep them clean. Well, I promised myself to explain it – *yet again*, and for the last time. So there it is. I suppose after this reprimand I'm free as never before.'

But he kept trying. 'My dear. We are comfortably if not happily situated. Why doubt such a simple thing? Doubt something complicated or arcane. Doubt voltaics. Or etherics, by god! You were raised in a privileged world, where treasure was thrown open by a whispered wish. This philosophy of yours, how resistant is it to the consequences of reality?'

'Fashion rode roughshod over my claims but reality upheld them. Handled particularly, culture assumes a position where reality is invasive.'

'Are we to have more lectures on freedom and consequence? This is the socialism of the Incas. It doesn't mesh with our nation's gears. Perhaps in Russia, where the gravity is heavier and the people slower.'

'We all live inhibited, numbed by the specifics of whatever class we inhabit. It's all one corner, when viewed by a free soul. One detailed little cloister cradling all that waste and tragedy. You own the other half of this truth. You know it. Or you used to know. What happened? It seems you've been sworn to stupidity. Can a thinking man sink lower? Have you sold your soul at public auction?' She drew a breath. 'There, father. I have been hysterical for you, and where has it got us?'

Lord Shafto was clearly unconvinced by this

recital, but seemed to receive some obscure signal from within himself. He peered toward the observation windows. Then he put a silencing finger to his lips and approached the large cast-iron crucifix on the wall, flipping it over. In the opposite wall, the massive baronial fireplace began to turn like a fairground ride. It locked to a halt at ninety degrees, offering an entry into something. Shafto gestured and she followed. She was glimpsing a warm memory through the gap, and then she entered it.

The facade closed behind them. Here was a hidden library bejewelled with books. Octagonal wood panelling and a silence as round as a ball. Pickled chairs and treacly cupboards. Printed matter smelling of matches, opulently bound and creased like shoes. She remembered an incandescent experience of clandestine texts, a summer heart brimming in its own curiosity. To some minds, ink is a narcotic. This lush peace, in which books of prinkopoetics and carnagenia leaned against the logick works of Laplace and Thomas Reid, had given her the sense of being in league with herself. There was the porcelain crab on the mantel and the conch shell like a chicken fossil. A high window poured with sallow light and a lower rose window formed a red and blue porthole onto the front drive. There was the dusty potbellied stove and a scarab-like copper control panel studded with small crank-wheels. In a photogram, a child sat stuffed full of other people's smiles.

'All your old research on pocket vortexes is in the cupboard,' said her father. Now that they were backstage his face had a very home-made look. The last few minutes had not been kind to him. 'I believe you've put all this away in a corner, in your mind, because you never speak of her, but you, your mother and I would read together here. The three of us reading, and it seemed to me the most perfect thing. The sun coming in that window, making squares of light. You especially liked Joseki's *Midas Pig*, the one that runs amok freezing everyone like a gorgon. Some of our richest memories are of small heavens tucked away in quiet. The days when the scratch of a quill seemed to make hypocrites flinch. Innocent days really. When Alice died I couldn't come in here for years, and had it sequestered, as you see. You were still young, and times had changed. Thinking's worse than murder – and the wrong feeling? I wanted to protect you. You were always quick to consideration.'

She thought of the years she had seen the pelting atoms in everything but told nobody. 'I suppose in me the condition was already much advanced.'

'And amid such danger. A world where morality is mere signage and the flimsiest principles are prone to inflammation. You could never seem to do enough to make up for it. You were so hard on yourself.'

'Would you protect me by having me deny who I was? Pretending you're unscathed is a wretched way to live, father.'

'I know.' He sighed deeply. 'Oh, this is a perplexing business I daresay.'

Sophie picked up a copy of *Volvadine*, the story of a traveller who falls into the burrow system of a young conservative and returns with tales of a topsy-turvy world. Its cover was shockingly familiar, a nursery-rhyme illustration of a clumsy creature with gates for wings and a moon for a head.

'My recent visits here have been lonely,' said Shafto. 'Just me and an uninvited wasp or two. You've given me quite a scare. You can well imagine how worried I was. I've slept like a galley slave when I slept at all.'

'I'm sorry, papa. I wish you could have seen the idea. There's nothing like it built today. It was so good I almost kept it a secret. But in this vacuum I had to let it bleed a little.'

'Whatever it was, it'll die where it lies won't it? Why spoil it with talking and conclusions? It'll rot for lack of necessity. Things make sense on a timescale we can't really register. Life and its vanished instructions, incomplete under the stars – ours not to reason why, Zozo. Fools and fiends erode especially slowly. It's as if they're laminated and we have to wait till they get brittle.'

'So that's what you're counting on.'

'Yes, child. Equanimity – it's not a resolve but... more of a daily lapse.'

'Yes, a falling back. You want to replace understanding with contentment. Oh, papa. "If each angel asks a question it fills the night", remember? And most never make it past the darkness.'

'We always had a hard time keeping up with that runaway brain. You had a habit of tasting eternity before you earned it. Strangers couldn't pass you on the street without you telling them the truth.' He laughed. 'I try. Because you shouldn't have to go through the truth alone. I've even read Feste. He accrues truths the way another might scrape barnacles from a slimy hull.' He took down a copy of *The Boring Culprit*.

'Shall I sign it?'

Sophie scribbled Emmanuel Feste's name on the author page. Her father seemed dazed. 'I told you, papa, my bones are my own. The first and last letters of the common alphabet are more fissile than you know. Why else keep them apart?'

'It's a long horizon for those who apply this sort of knowledge,' he said quietly. 'Is such heroism found in nature?'

'Yes, I think so.'

'Yes, perhaps it is,' he said, looking tired, and slumped down in an old armchair. 'As usual you're right, or something.'

'What can you tell me about Brewster's new towers? I've seen the land deeds.'

'Towers? He's bought a bunch, I don't know any more. Don't interfere with Brewster, child. He'll be picking you out of his teeth before bedtime.'

'Why do you think so?'

'He's a thoroughgoing bastard, that's all. His conclusions are so weightless I dismissed them at first. Now I'm not so sure. Says he wants nothing from me, so of course I'm on the alert. It seems like the components of his morality reconfigure every few seconds. Perfect evasion. Hark at me talking about evasion – that's what he sells isn't it?'

'Thankfully, scripts and masks burn at a similar rate. Let me prove it to you.'

'I'll admit, such a daunting blessing terrifies me. Retribution so long delayed may as well be an assault out of the blue. You won't be understood.'

'To those without memory, everything comes

out of the blue. Their beliefs are supported like the frailest towers in our town – by the others on either side. But those who can think keep score.'

'Full blast on all cylinders eh? Ah, Zozo. If you're anything like me you'll do whatever it takes.' He was whispering now. He stood and opened a safe of walnut wood, retrieving a lug-heavy machine pistol. 'That's all any of us can do. You'll have one chance to strike. Careful, or this'll blast you to pulp.'

It felt like a fragile gift given to a child and put away until she was old enough to care for it properly. 'You are rather like Tom, papa. As the differences between us got thicker, they better conducted a charge.'

'Well, it'll be a gala event I daresay. Just don't expect the next colour to be one you haven't seen before. And remember,' he added furtively, 'if someone looks enigmatic and tells you you're "asking the wrong question", it's okay to belt 'em in the chops.'

'I will. Thank you, papa.'

They embraced, and Sophie was crying.

'Let's argue on the way out,' he suggested. 'Everyone must think we came to blows at the consultation. That detective lurks behind doors and can open them all. I thought I caught sight of her earlier. Remember the meticulous shouting match we had about atomic inversion? At the end you pushed me into some brambles.'

'I remember the altercation. It's one of my favourites.'

'Good. Grab a coat in the hall, it's snowing. Keep your chin up, it shallows the breath. Then there's hell to pay. Here we go.'

He opened the wall and Sophie strode out. He emerged behind her, blowing his stack. 'Won't you ever get out of here? You're innocent because you have the luxury to be so, at my expense! And when ascending, Jesus did not say "Up I go"!'

'If he was here he'd punch you right in the belly!'

'There's the door! It demands simplicity when it demands anything! Must I chase you out with every leg?'

'Spoken like a true elephant! I scoff at your velocity! Fat-headed fat-head! Goodbye!' And she closed the door with exceptional speed.

§

Dry, sour snow fell on the broad courtyard and its scattered assembly of man-sized chess figures in attitudes of combat. Nightjar, layered in black, stood against the back of a rampant iron knight. The snow had already covered the pear-coloured grass and capped the statuary, along with Nightjar's sooty stub of hair.

Sophie emerged from the Steel Tower, beleaguered by a winter coat. Nightjar showed herself, and stopped breathing. She was seeing Sophie in a moment of angelhood, phosphenes around her head like a penny assortment of minor raptures. Sophie was indifferent to her glory as a peacock ignores the mandala it carries. The girl walked right up to the Inspector, so beautiful, small and spectacular. It was lightning at eye level. She had been crying. Nightjar remembered a woozy dream she had had in which Sophie had a tiny padlock on each tear duct.

'You killed Tom,' Sophie said. 'The dullest hole can swallow a lion. You resemble the bloated bitch on our currency.'

'You disagree with me and it's making you unpleasant,' Nightjar replied breathlessly. 'You've led me a merry dance. Until your book befell me, that exacting tantrum you call *Truth's Flying Visit*. Your unregistered brainchild, I should say.' Almost as an afterthought, she took out her police-issue revolver and looked at it as if it were made of liquorice. The hand holding it was numb.

'And you want me to do what exactly? When acting momentous, you'd better have supporting evidence.'

'I'm authorised to suggest that you've been unduly influenced. Railroaded. Can I expect rationality in your present distress?'

As if they had agreed to have a battle, Sophie had levelled two firearms. In her right hand was a pink-handled ladies' pistolette barely bigger than a prawn and in the left a steam gun resembling a heavy hunk of industrial equipment. 'Your offer to diminish me is tempting, but I have you outgunned.'

'I assure you this drab little pistol will blast you from the lawn. If you had a larger imagination you'd appreciate what I'm offering.'

'If I had a larger imagination my head would vaporize. Yours too, my dear. You strike me as a show pony, spurred on to others' profit.'

'For all I know that might be true. Every bit of information I've imparted has since been compromised.'

'Of course. They'll stitch through you to their own pattern and leave an incoherent heart. Don't exert yourself, they don't really care.'

'I care.'

'People don't like to have their rules applied back to them. They'll have your skull for an ashtray. You're worth less to them than these big-mouthed lawn trophies father had sent down from Edinburgh. They're called gulptures I think.'

'It's all very picturesque. And I must say even togged up as a chimney sweep you're rather brilliant, like a bird or a' – Nightjar gulped – 'a vegetable.'

'Like it, do you?'

'It tells a tale, like ballet shoes in a tiger pit. I've been around a long time, Sophie, paying attention, and can assure you that your only safe option is to come in under my guard.'

'I'm sure that's the law: all forced perspective. I've scudded over its man-made promontories myself for a few years and have yet to discern any pattern but the gears of class and power. Investigate Brewster's power station. Or Terminal Tower. Do your job. Why arrest an anarchist? Might as well slip cuffs on a snowman.'

'Very well.' Nightjar remembered to raise the gun. 'Sophie Shafto, I am charging you –'

Nightjar felt a slashing heat at her back. Her vision scrambled and she was laying face-first in sharp snow. She rolled herself over. Sophie was gone. She could see only Albion's heatless sun, her own breath and the armoured knight, its sword lowered.

19

Parliament of Words

Brewster entered an office as dark and detailed as old suffering. He had seen Chancellor Swive from a distance, his face in a constant rear of disdain as if overpowered by his own prestige, but at close quarters the man was radiant with failings. Telegraphing a cleverness he did not possess, he shallowed within moments.

'You're a hard man to find, Swive, among the wriggling damned.' Brewster seated himself and glanced about at the décor. 'This is some room huh? "Letters lean together in the dark places of the law." And a chandelier with whiskers! Well, Chancellor, we've never met but you're about to find out. I'm hardly overjoyed to be dealing with your kind. The current crisis demands it. You heard the news?'

'Your rooms at the top of the Consolidated tower. These radicals and their presumptuous explosions!'

'Quite the bang. The device was in a hatbox,

I'm told, delivered a few days ago by a pretty rum-looking postman. I was at work and lucky for Daisy she's on the other side of the planet and so also out of range. The incompetence rings a bell doesn't it? The Rook up to his old tricks. In any case a whole bunch of Rook calling cards were found scattered at the scene, fresh-printed – identical to the one with Talion. A clear sign he's got a lot up his sleeve. Thanks to you everyone knows about unmutuals and their ominous make-believe. Various malevolent forces are bandied about, many not well-known enough to be misunderstood, but the pre-eminent nuisance is the Rook. As godsends go he's a corker. By denouncing him so broadly in all his aspects I fear you get no traction on the logical mind, but that hardly matters.'

'Yes, I'm pretty familiar with the Rook and his aimless intrigues. It suits me that he's generally pictured in a storm-drain lair, sharpening his chin.'

'Yes, yes, the Grand Convolution and those who profit by it. But the way you do it's like squeezing a chicken for an egg. Orthodox deception's for the birds. End-to-end rivalry without ventilation or interest, that's the future. That way they're born pre-thwarted. Parched with incoherence.'

Swive was looking so academically appreciative it was clear he didn't know what he was hearing.

'Chaos, Chancellor – channel it why don't you! What we need is the leaden oblivion of the law. Bring a jackal to heel and you may lose a leg. But a unifying threat that's harmless?'

Swive showed no inclination to understand him.

'Look at this.' Brewster took out the bound screed which Nightjar had left on his desk. '*Truth's Flying Visit*. It's a pressure leak, Chancellor. I'm an engineer and I know. This and books like it are inflammatory. This one here is practically the Rook's bible! Listen: "We strive to individuate a mistake so as not to acknowledge the universal error." The stuff's poison! And you only have to think about molasses to get sticky, Rodge. It's true. Every anarchist ever apprehended has been the owner of at least five books. Five! Remember 1649? Quarrels erupt on arable land and the next thing you know you're hiding in a sty.'

'So the song is, reading is dangerous and the unlettered, ignorant peasants are getting out of hand.'

'You contradict yourself repeatedly, Rodge, and I'm loving it. Like talking to ten different people. That's the game. Point a dozen different ways with authority. Regulate them limb from limb. Oh, you're a crafty one, Chancellor!'

With a sniff of offended dignity, Swive asked

Brewster what he proposed.

'Here's the idea,' Brewster stated, 'from my private stock. A combined amnesty and burning of all books, starting here in your great capital. Emergency legislation. A gangway discussion decides a lot. In this ordained context it shouldn't be controversial to suggest a blaze in every square and garden. Say they're burning the seeds of revolution and other phantom outrages. Bastards walk among us. A threat and the easy resolve not to recognise its cause. Common incomprehension – that's a uniting force, while containing no substance. The very thing I love and use, Chancellor. No content atall, uniting the nation!'

'I disagree. What counts is how long a mistake is sustained. History, sir, has a function.'

'You're right, the principles of inertial error use long spans of history, but it can function in as little as a fortnight, I assure you. Cheap chicanery is as sure a link as iron. A man can't be made to climb a ladder if it leads to something better. But if you aim it downward? Ever a trapdoor to something lower. Assign it a luxury slogan and you're home free.'

'You won't convince my colleagues.'

'I can do without others' judgement, we all can. Does anyone ever say "That condemnation of yours was a real lifesaver"? I listen only to those who agree with me. I find them convincing. In this case I consulted with five people of like mind, and they agreed with my analysis. In fact they were creased with laughter in my bathroom mirrors. No, keep me out of it. This pretty idea's for you to present at some nocturnal assembly. It'll surprise everyone that you thought of anything. You, a man made entirely of cheeks! Let's face it, stripped of pedigree you're a pudding, Rodge. That's right, a suction eel and, when dead, a fistful of drooling plugs. But eels are bold enough, or a thing like that wouldn't survive would it? Your mind, and its famous lack of scope, can be stretched like taffy but to little advantage if the ingredients stay the same. And you know what? I like it. But my plan is the sort of thing you could present before the crown heads of Hades! Burn the books? Most people would be surprised they weren't burnt already! Get a few biddable luminaries to back you up. They'll sign off on your fortune-telling because it's convenient. And what could be better calculated to shatter everyone's attention? It has an upright self-righteousness combined with a celebratory air. Give it all the pomp and tedium of a parade. Drag a wheeled dreadnought down Rag Street and do a march-past of four thousand badgers if you like, it doesn't matter. Remember the Great Exposition?

An empire festival under one big unanimous sky! Thronging and fawning. Vapour and vestments. They'll swallow the idea fins and all. Put a buckle round a rose, smart guy. It'll be smooth sailing any way you slice it. People will point at you in the street and think the energy well spent though they're near to dying.'

In Swive's eye was a glimmer of misplaced triumph. 'It's true the endorsements of society can be timed like the tides. And after what I've said about agitators I'm validated by every upheaval.'

Brewster winked roguishly. 'Now that's shrewd. Your secret's safe with me, Rodge. The Rook and his outrageous exploits, smashing our times! Shooting a coot in a savoury garden! Spearhead this edict and you'll no longer be seen as the guy who stands around like a trumpet monkey, a pet of statute, superfluous under pressure, inadequate, not equipped and so forth. Adulation, buster! You'll have your day and eat it! As the French say, it's a law easier passed in emergency than in cold blood. And while you're at it you can go to town, sprinkle it with one harrowing proviso after another, whatever you like. Number it, it'll look like a system. Then it's off to the races.'

'Oh, details. I employ a benumbed cleric for that. But do we need a law, when we have a trend?'

'I hate to say it but even today there are a handful over whom fashion has no power. They're barely aware of it. We're blowing smoke through a spyglass here, buckaroo – the sort of lie that rolls back and forth like thunder, increasing returns, an automatic sort of miracle. No-one ever ingratiated themselves using the truth. At worst there'll be a day or two of shooting and cannibalism, we'll profess surprise in lockstep and then things will settle down. Now, the proposal needs to be made the right way. Say it with an ominous look and they'll just waste time unpacking it. Do it with the empty look you've got now, kind of like a moron. Lofty and pleased – that's thin stuff. It means barely anything. With the right preparation you can deliver ten vapid homilies in the first minute. Then get folksy, then no-nonsense.'

'I know how to give a speech. Haven't you been keeping up to date with my outbursts? The last one was about my "Bludgeon a Curmudgeon" campaign.'

'I was at the back of the hall when you outlined the pro-phossy legislation last year. A very intricate bit of negligence, I noticed. Kudos! You didn't cheat and you even restored the obstacles. But your speech was trash. I had to refurbish those hints and tell everyone you were certain. And would it have killed you to be audible? They'll entertain your ordinances if they interest in some way. It wouldn't hurt to include some colour, some pazazz. Arrive suddenly. The sudden appearance of even the most boring thing can make an impression. Belligerent vainglory better have a punchline. There's more of them than you. A rhyme leads to lazy conclusions, try something like that.'

'"What must be done I think you know; And I don't mean jump naked into a vat of dough."'

'Good, but it could be better. How about "We don't want a mutiny; Nor any scrutiny". A notion like this needs a drawbridge at both ends. At that point it'll take only one person to bulge his eyes for everyone to start doing it. Insist on a bolster, you're a short man. And remember to emphasise that inaction could have deadly consequences, now or later, to us or someone else. It's beautiful, pure augment, conveying no information.'

'I'm not so sure.'

'Well, I could take this to Sir Outland.'

'You don't want him. He's in hot water for holding a hen aloft and saying he loved it. He's finished. What'll you pay me?'

'One molecule from my face. I've done my research as to your tastes, Rodge. It's either this or a diplomatic post on a penguin island. Though judging by your tastes, you might like that. Put my proposition and the dividends it yields are dead in a dead hand. Well suited to you, Chancellor. Keep in mind the upcoming election or "switcheroo" as we call it back home, where the aim is to degrade the electorate until they're thinking by smell alone. You'll ride in on an inferno of approval and survive in stagnant majesty for another few years.'

'I'm sure I don't know what you mean.'

'I know how it works around here. Kiss a statue, make a wish.' He grinned conspiratorially. 'Mum's the word.'

Swive held his chin to think with more foundation and seemed to come up with nothing he liked. 'It seems you have me between a rock and the deep blue sea.'

'You mean the devil and a hard place. But your convictions appear to be stacked like slices of bread, capable of being squashed down as a whole or eaten one at a time.'

'I believe what you're describing is a sandwich.'

'A sandwich, yes. Well, thousands crouch on command don't they?'

Swive muttered to indicate a lack of definite information, but offered no further objections.

Brewster stood. 'I find after all that you're my kind of man, Chancellor. A working model of a man, without content. Stock detail. Take my tip, buy Amerikaana bonds.' He smirked. 'I'll leave you to your deliberations.'

The howling empties of that bloodless meeting had taken their toll, even on Brewster. As he left, Swive was grasping his own head like a football.

20

All or Nothing

Standing at a wooden easel in her cluttered parlour, Nightjar thought about a revolutionary at the end, the hunted look of rapture in his eyes, his face dented as a snubbed saviour. Something came to a close there, it was clear. But the Rook was the sort of rebel icon who died note-for-note and right on time. His was at best a lifetime tantalized by readiness and invigorated by the world's opposition. She was disappointed to have been a part of it.

She had come at this case sideways and got embedded like a thorn. Oblique striations created something otherwise, rich and thick with the flavours of variants. And for a time she could not remove herself.

Now, the case had simply leafed apart around her, fluttering loose in a sort of easy scorn.

The beauty of it was Emmanuel Feste, whose ink-blue heart and secret brain were just a part of

Sophie, an angel sweating gold. Her hypernatural mind, blank skin and hair black as the compass on a blond map. Nightjar remembered the first book she had fallen in love with. The dragon treacle of that summer was so intense, the stench of worry and youth. The book had clenched her into honeycells and kept her alive. Nothing took more resolve than to inhabit the improbable life. Yet its treasure became easily available when she ceased to need acknowledgement. No resting on laurels that are never given.

She scrutinised the canvas. What she had laid down so far resembled the ocean, a glittering fuss seemingly designed to conceal crabs and fish.

There was a loud rapping at the door. She opened it to find Lord Shafto in full bluster, dressed in the grand mercantile style and brandishing a cane topped with a cog-head. But in his eyes she saw real distress. Like a drowned man, his own gas had brought him at last to the light. He pushed past her into the room. 'By will alone, I enter!'

'Must you erupt into a room so, like a walrus late for lunch? Why are you here?'

'A hankering for convention. You gave me your word and I believed you. Your promises are gone to ruin. Sophie's still missing, I'm subject to tawdry scrutiny and this alleged Method of yours strikes me as rubbish. All you do is rattle what you find into a different order. A sparrow does the same and at least has a nest to show for it.'

'It's you who expects everyone to believe Sophie fell for some hairpin dogma. Was caught into a passing skirmish, the wrong crowd with the wrong expertise. Very obviously she's the mastermind of her own fate.' Nightjar returned to her easel. 'But then hardly a day goes by when I don't feel cheated of the truth.'

'Confound it all, I don't care what you think and we'll see about that! I drag out here to Tower bloody Hamlets to beg one sign of progress and you sport with me! You've sneered down your arms at me from the start, you brickhouse crone!'

'A lion will seem to sneer as it worries your head off but it's only doing a job. I am suspended, Lord Shafto. For clarity. I'm sorry you came all this way for nothing.'

Shafto regarded the Inspector with dismay. 'Well, the very idea. Suspended you say? How do you square this with your outburst the other day? Down to the studs, you said.'

'The state's shy of its studs. As for my Method, the greatest convergences occur without ceremony. Perhaps because they occur within. In any case, the pattern of their results becomes evident in retrospect, and that's where the criminal law generally operates. You come in here purple with inconvenience and the velveteen tribulations of having too much money. Is there any reason I should understand you?'

'I don't care about money. Guessing all night – that's my life now!'

'It's everybody's. But take consolation in this. Sophie is a pure gold, nailed-on genius. You know of course that she's Emmanuel Feste? Compression's not the half of it. I met her publisher, a literary sawbones who once specialised in miniaturised "knuckle books" which could be placed between the halves of a walnut and thrown at people. He has gone completely insane.'

'I was just recently told about the Feste books. But are they really a threat? Who is it that thinks Sophie's thoughts in their head? Do her ideas have friends in reality?'

'You assert that she's taken up with a band of brothers.'

'What does a group mean? What about satanists? They worship a cat sat up on its haunches.'

'A goat I think, Lord Shafto.'

'Ah, cat, goat, on its haunches, in a crib, it's a bad business either way. She's gone fish-blinking mad, that's the tale I'm telling the papers now. A regrettable clear-sightedness, a softening of the character. It fits with the Lambing and so on. I wasn't especially lying when I said I didn't know what she was about. But I thought we could chalk it up to rabies and move on.'

'She's an heiress, a lady. For her kind, contrition is thin, the barest procedure. But if she does something of interest, it will be different.' Nightjar looked at her canvas for clues. 'It doesn't matter if it has any long-term effect. I'd be surprised if it did. Tradition has it that after a revolution, the option of true freedom is presented and quickly removed again before it even casts a shadow.'

'I know, it's like one of those meals that's set on fire but has to be blown out anyway before you eat it. Doesn't matter about me, I can take anything. I eat a healthy three cigars a day. Iron constitution. But Sophie's determined to – I don't know – go out in a flash of blazes or something, at one of Brewster's towers. She'll be choffing up blood. Then under the ground, a scrum of fidgeting bugs and she's done! Done! Inspector, I've reached the end of my chain! I don't know what to do! She stormed into the Steel making sense to high heaven! She's always been that way! Do you know at the age of five she whacked a vicar in the face with a frying pan?'

'An act with no familiar implications.'

'I know, but I think it was because we had her reading and then forbade it. Waywardness requires a pre-agreed normality. Disgrace needs structure and structure needs teaching. It needn't mean anything.'

'To invite against. I suppose it sets up a tension.'

Shafto seemed to be coming apart. He was scavenging at his own face. 'Pity the soul who's wise at the outset, Inspector. Time passes hard. And when your upbringing is an archive, everything feels like the future. I think it's the parents' sad lot to lay track only to find they're wrong on both sides. From early days she had a theory about a set of societal dimensions arranged to keep the bullseye floating always behind us.'

'"Where life is offered up like a bill, not a meal, the effect is a series of expensive trivialities under a borrowed sky."'

'Well that's to be expected in a baying outcast but is bloody disconcerting in a child. As for your laws, the boundaries are so dull she rarely noticed them.'

'It doesn't surprise me. All the nobler sanctions are obvious and don't need to be written – the rest is a chore without nutritious content or a knot to be undone. But what else will we do with our time? Face facts? We live in houses to split the situation.'

'But that's the point! That's Sophie! And if truth controlled the world, its conclusion would be reached within hours. Minutes! A world in which everything is infernally apparent!'

'Sounds like paradise, Lord Shafto. It sounds honest. Tell the truth. If you haven't tried the experiment before, you may find there's something uncanny about the result.'

'An imposed division always corresponds to a fear, is that the song? Matter all of a piece can't be sorted out and water's the same upside down.'

'A table's bald but nobody pities it, Mr Shafto. Categories do clarify in the short term, and can even be useful if employed at a good angle. The question is, which is to be master. Or shall we get swamped and embrace what deceives us? Look at this.' She gestured at the painting with her brush. 'A trillion contained fanaticisms – is it a rich heaven or a toxic hell?'

He looked diffidently at the mass of colours. 'It'd depend on the trillions' willingness to coexist, obviously.'

'Obviously. The ocean has been racking up countless waves of sundry variation in an experiment it shows no sign of concluding. As many injustices as grains of sand. And the tide is erasure, not justice.'

'I've always thought the land doesn't stand a chance against the sea. It can't end any other way. But it's still natural for us to fight it like Canute.

Some sort of order. Have you talked to Brewster? He's a slippery one. Wouldn't be surprised if he could jettison his legs like a lizard. I've stood cheek-by-quivering-jowl with his type and he's suspect as a pawn shop bugle.'

'Yes, I spoke to him, when allowed to interrupt. I've learned that what you see through a rend in the fabric of a lie won't always be true, because people are layered. But in the case of Brewster, he flips opinions so often he seems to annihilate the integrity of the surrounding atmosphere. Shreds it. He strives to be meaningless. Empty.'

Shafto sagged into a chair and looked utterly miserable. 'Aye, he certainly gives outer space a run for its money. What did Talion say about him?'

'That the answer lies in the soil. I'm still absorbing that response. Brewster is a man of the modern age, really. In past times he could set up as a beacon of insolence in a meek expanse. Now he need be no more than a vacuum point in an empty void. The bar has been buried. You hail from up north I believe, Lord Shafto?'

'Crankston, a town held together by rust. Not so much as a jelly sixpence to my name. Poverty's easy to accomplish – all the world'll help. I thought vapour engines were pleasant and useful. Still do. I knew the future was mine the first time I saw a boiler stack on a bricky's cart. I've led the world since the Exposition. But things move on. Kettle cars were one thing, now I see carts with the heat flukes of the Sparks company like the puncture wounds of a bloody great vampire. In tax I've paid a king's ransom for reassurance and now look what's happened. I'm the bulging embodiment of steam power and the papers say I'm a hog. What a damned nuisance. Weeping's what it used to be, at least.'

'This might interest you.' She took down a pasteboard cumdach from a shelf and slipped from it a book with a hammered copper cover. It smelt of spices and soot. '*The Lux Atlas*, a text which everyone perhaps mischievously misunderstood. When most people believe the world is flat, Lux the Sailor goes around the globe and encounters his homeland again, which he concludes is a crafty replica – a belief supported by the fact that its inhabitants think he is an imposter. He sails on a second time and encounters another false version of his homeland, and so on. An inquiry was conducted and the book pulped. All but this copy.'

Shafto looked slowly amazed. 'I never thought I'd see one in my lifetime.'

'Listen to this: "The law is an important step toward understanding human nature, or even preventing it." Were you always a reader?'

'Oh, a book's a trap in the shape of a rose – clump and you're all surrounded by veiny walls and heady fumes. That's the devilish part of it. Yes, I read it all. *The Silver Germ*, *Roy Tumbler's Registry*, *The Brothers Orchard*, the lot. Victor Magnitude, Rossum, Hermine, and even Mustana.'

'I have Rossum's *Book of the Machines* here somewhere, and Hinton. Plus *The Rain Bible*, *The Spike Bible*, *The Craw Bible*. Craw proposed a god who upended this universe and ran off. And that we should tolerate it till we're discarded down its winking throat. And Rain spoke of an internal organ without a name, candy-clawed and ghostly – the one that knows everything.'

'So she did. So she did.'

'You should know that the Chancellor of the Circuit plans to propose a crisis. It seems all the bad ideas come to life again out of obscure personal urgency. The Crown already supports it in outline.'

'Oh, godswallop. We've all heard the rumour that she's three years dead and the thing on the throne is an automaton. That cogwheel madonna plays chess like the Turk, with Albion on the board.'

'Well, dead or alive, she's a dutiful puppet and her reign carefully curated.'

'This is sedition.'

'Yes. Wouldn't you have expected it to feel

more exciting? The proposed ordinance is a book burning. Things were lax when books were merely baffling or unfashionable – suspect in some amorphous way. The decision has now been taken to portray them as dangerous. There will be many bonfires, and those who are there will not remember they ever took part. It will be casual and commonplace. They'll forget the names of those who raised a hand.'

'But they're not dangerous,' said Shafto wearily. 'Books stumble upon the truth over and over, stating it openly, to no effect.'

'Yes, the ideal wouldn't really require the burning of books – no-one would be interested in the first place. Something else is at play. It's not simple revulsion at the existence of the other. Books have become self-fertile. I've seen it first-hand. And there's nothing more annoying than those we reject thriving without us.'

'A burning. I don't care for that at all.'

'The strangeness of the mob is its ability to magnetize absolutely to a truth or to a lie. It won't know the difference until there's blood in its wallet. I'm told I should take such stupidity at face value, but I always suspect – I can't say why – that they are pretending. That there is some motive for them not to understand.'

'You think a person so meticulously unreasonable may be play-acting?'

'I don't know. I change my mind about it all the time. Intelligence is mental territory laid down, which to that person seems to cover everything. Idiots have a smaller territory, which to them seems to cover everything. Within their everything, their acts make perfect sense. Even for the most intelligent it's forever incomplete. At the moment intelligence has descended to the point that basic common sense is mistaken for prescience. I'm exhausted even thinking about it.'

'I want to believe you care about Sophie and her wellbeing. If I could save her I'd do it in a heartbeat and for roughly the same money. Is there anything you can do? You solved the Sulletine murder!'

'A gun hidden in a melon, that's easy. Have you heard of the Whyland case? He did it with the same necktie he would wear to his confession. Even at its most inventive homicide is boring. It's never anything more than homicide. Whyland was sent to prison victorious. A man may hang cunning from the gallows. Others outlive the penalty.'

'You chased down the Rook didn't you?'

'You know he posed as Percy Valentine, the poet who thought behind a red velvet rope?'

'Yes, one idiot disguised as another. Damned clever I suppose. Allow me again to ask your pardon for the accident with the lawn ornament. Who could have predicted it would be defective.'

'I accept your apology. Kindness is one of the last real surprises we can hope for. That front sweep of yours is rather like the yard of an anvil farmer.' In fact she didn't mind the healing scar across her back. It would be a reminder-wound so sweet to stroke, if she could reach it.

Shafto looked so dejected that Nightjar felt compelled to reassure him. What could she say?

'Do you remember Boileau? "In mistaken times, contrariness is the fount of all goodness." Boileau was wrong about that. Goodness should exist irrespective of the times. How it engages may depend on circumstance. And I believe Sophie is good. I'll see what I can do for her, Lord Shafto.'

After Shafto had left, Nightjar took down a volume of Margaret Cavendish. There was a concept called the Vauxhall Principle, which dealt with mental acceleration and the point at which the brain starts palpably scorching. At first it seemed to Nightjar that Sophie had been forewarned so tenaciously for so long, it had made a thing compelling. That she had called its bluff and reversed herself, banging open an explosion that knocked pieces of road into the sky. It came to her quietly that Sophie was neither surrounded by influence nor allowed her focus to be controlled by the act of surrounding it. A hermit crab is at home in a dog skull and won't understand it's a social clanger. The greatest happiness is immune to considerations of prestige, as the fire of approval burns the bad and the good.

§

They knew him as a man whose brain was hemmed with apology and dead in the middle. He went about with a solemnity comical for its lack of content. The fellow preceding him had spoken high-flown misconceptions like a drowsy sultan, merging with the chamber's venerable staleness. Swive stepped up to the dispatch box and started shouting better than they expected. The speech was a swamp from which its one item of fact could rear unexpectedly, covered in ancient snot.

'Revolution, an impulse of unknown origin. These scofflaws, feeble and dangerous, bow their heads only when preparing to ram us. Raised on reproach fables and cock-a-hoop with bloodlust, the revolution they describe sounds almost quaint. They say everyone should think for themselves, and then create a committee to enforce it! But make no mistake, the most effective superstitions have no moving parts. Anarchism is for today's purposes defined as a reckless agency of chaos and no finer meaning. The anarchist! Snuffling in rain, waiting outside royalty – don't pity him for the wrong reason. He is distributing bombs to the poor! And rioters are like radishes – for the right price they're anyone's. These ragged elites, comprised of outcasts, inveterate noticers and those who are valiant against the very floor that supports them, are shameless, scandalous, ruinously expensive. Organised revolution wants justice to be done on a human timescale. Nature has other ideas, and coincidentally so do we. If there is one among us who does not say to himself of a morning, "No consequence today, Lord", I give that man leave to pound me on the arse with a paddle. A pox on parity. Will we allow ourselves to be rushed by some crowd of lively malcontents calling themselves the Mayday Syndicate or the Pumption League? Who are these people?

'It has been my duty as Chancellor of the Circuit to keep track of such organisations. In the course of monitoring their mad and interminable correspondence I have discovered that they worship a god with ink on its hands. They are book eaters, one and all! I have here one such tract, sarcastically titled *Truth's Flying Visit*. Allow me to read a passage at random: "The collectivisation of taste is a red flag. A crowd can act without reason or honest passion. Shall we blame this on a demon?" My Lords this reasoning leaves me weak and amazed! This book is a plague ship that should never have reached our pretty shore, and those who traffic in such texts are a contamination of our national trends. That these cargo cults englory them is hardly surprising. And I have established that the Rook regards such printed edicts without discernment, accepting them unexamined in a rapture near to bibliomancy. The Rook, whose bombastic marvels are of interest to us all. The Rook, that notorious fanatic who manipulated the face of the First Earl of Penbroke while that honourable gentleman slept, so that when he awoke his nose had been turned inside-out like a glove! A glove, my friends! The Rook, who cavorted naked upon a mechanical ant! The Rook, who executed our beloved mercantile ghoul Aksel Talion in a happy garden, his tenth murder in this style in as many of the southern counties! Indeed the Rook and others like him have vanquished upward of a thousand people in cold blood and without so much as a by-your-leave. And he himself lays claim to the recent bombing of Brewster Consolidated which was delivered in a gaudy hatbox designed to eject from inside it, and I quote from the *Times*, "a twisting storm with sick yellow flashes inside and a bonus afterglow like a sunbeam". I need hardly point out the parallels to the text I recited earlier! Book eaters absorb information at a speed which better nurtures clarity. We cannot allow such orgies of calm consideration, not to mention those voodoo frenzies known as reading circles! Does anyone doubt that these texts, some centuries old, are diseased and malignant? In this connection, I move for the immediate adoption of more energetic measures. I propose this generalised fear be mandated into law and that all books should be presented and destroyed by fire.'

There were several nervously overloud shouts of approval.

'Our troops stand in a state of readiness that resembles constipation and we've a police force capable of anything. This public menace and the dog's apocrypha they use for guidance? Let's see how they sit and ponder when they find themselves on the business end of a holocaust!

'The question of legality is beyond the scope of this outburst. Everywhere there is a cry for immediate action and in this one case we would do well to listen. You will agree that I have resorted to this conclusion not without an absence of logic. Let us not attend to those who wish to intrigue. I give this specialised outcry not for personal glory, but have been assured that in the national interest it is prudent to give a raucous sleigh-ride of a speech endorsing emergency measures and I am here – arm, leg and torso – to do precisely that. A hippo's ears will flutter like the wings of a swallow but I shall not be deterred from decrying everything into even the slackest of faces. If you can summon one microscopic piece of bygone conviction, send a message! These measures mark a new and more lucrative chapter for the nation and its empire! All animals join our advantage, hoorah!'

In a rare show of cross-party unity, everyone peered at one another for validation. Swive looked as smug as a tugboat.

After the aye vote, the First Earl of Penbroke approached Swive for a private word. He wore the imperial flag over his lower face. 'There's not much to the idea,' he snorted, 'it's basically a cape on wheels, am I right?'

'Yes,' said Swive.

21

The Treasure Itself

In Lovelace Park, a railed enclosure had been set up on the lawn. Passersby dropped books over the side without slowing or looking, as though unaware of their actions. It reminded Jonah of the nose steam rules, designed to distance people from any suspicion of internal warmth. He was sitting next to Sophie on a floral iron bench, close enough to be within her cherry sherbet chemistry. After all the hiding and grudging of the last few days, he was still abuzz to be next to her mind. She was sumptuously disguised in widow's weeds, her face hidden behind a mourning veil. A black knapsack of explosives completed the outfit. Jonah could feel every detail of the scene glittering against him.

It seemed a clench had loosened in Sophie. She pointed in the sunlight. 'That little bridge was built in a more jovial and reckless age. See the pink monkeys? It's such a nice day.'

'Tradition states that there are seven angels ranged along any major bridge. Only three are charged with stopping suicides. The rest don't do anything. On a day like this I can appreciate the sarcasm of a well-appointed public park. The clatter of tin petticoats! I can feel the colour blushing back into the city.'

'I can't, quite, despite the sunshine. With enough priming you can feel almost anything under any circumstance, can't you? I doubt a child in a chimney is seeing much colour. An enclosure of situated errors is as good as you'll find here. People leave mistakes, and generations of people have been here before us. All the pickled years won't tell anything but a story. But I don't want to put you back into a brown study about enslavement.'

'Aren't you plotting a new story?'

'Yes. The scar on the cherry is that I won't belong in the future I create. Do you think I *want* to be right, Jonah? What will become of the world if I am?'

'Are you sure of your plan? Perhaps with someone so fathomlessly empty a headlong assault is unwise.'

'We dream of some molten black villain to simplify our choices. If we're very lucky we're given one. I don't think looking-glasses are a dead end. I just think none of these phenomena we've seen are causes, they're all effects of the same thing. The unacknowledged drive to not quite be. Nothing cures the cause, apparently. Brewster just amplifies and uses it. Of course all those printed books went wild. The real stuff always happens where nobody is looking and it got to the point where almost no-one was. In a culture so resolutely dull the colour has to leak through somewhere. The saying of the same thing repeatedly strengthens it for some, decreases its power for others. I've been asking myself, are my acts an interruption or a contribution to trance? And which is worth more? I mean a trance so steadfast that one part of it supports another, the whole keeping aloft through internal collaboration. Only a few find themselves unglamoured, as though fully awake during surgery, and it's agony, as you know. This particular society is a crisscross pantomime of bewildered ghosts and complacent demons. When I was a child every morning was like having a screaming Punch puppet bite my face. It's hard to find belonging in something so wrong.'

Jonah knew better than most how unhelpful it was to have one's burden clearly illuminated. For a man of his mind, clarity merely put agonies in alphabetical order, a headache that could teach nothing more but remained for years. Each night the stars were a timid blessing, eaten from all sides, and every day the sun rose to light a billion excruciating precisions. He was continually consumed by his own power source and it was an endless one. 'If this is an Adjusted World, as Carpstein theorised, then what we think dull, other worlds might take for high novelty. Our dullest conversation might to them seem intolerably lush or arcane. Those must be very dull worlds indeed.'

'I know how it is, Jonah. The mind overflows its banks. With the certainty that there's something next to this which is better and fizzing with joy. It's what the Vivid Age played on and makes this age so terrible. When everything is owned, everything will die. A stiff assemblage of perfections, how's that for a nurturing environment? So different from the fabled rowdiness of antiquity.'

Jonah thought about the carnival figure of the Troy Clown and his luminous derangement. Icon of the sixties, Fool of Feasts, Clown of the Revels, Trickster Angel, Cassian Jaspers, Mr Clowd, Alan – he was all these and a medicinal troubadour doing purple magic in hot daylight and other miraculous hi-jinx. Could he really have had a perforated head that was constantly discharging perfumed outrage? Some said he was lost in a kissed-out blowhole of eternity. Others said he subsided into his own legend with a final, incomprehensible injunction: 'Let the orchard swell and the rain never end.' Those who cared had torn him into souvenirs like a saint.

'But it is a fable,' Sophie went on. 'You can shout nostalgia into the face of the earth and vibrate a small width of clay. Much good may it do you. Like a lightning hit I'll illuminate them against their bloody will. I daresay I won't survive it, Jonah. I've sent Eaglet into the country. We've nearly reached the end. Aren't you glad?'

'The planet without you. Not really.'

'You can hardly say it's unexpected.'

A yard-wide gull pushed off, bored with their talk. Jonah leant back and looked at the sky. A loose anatomy of clouds drifted open, then slowly and strangely closed again. 'Listen, Sophie, you surely know that I love you. And it's true I want to scarf your brain like marmalade, but I would have more than that. I could climb every inch of you like a honey tree.'

'And "awake nude on an oyster reef, ticking with electricity", I know,' she said gently, smiling. 'The mind's tongue stretches to make contact. This intellectual love of ours exchanges a substance others can't see, an acceleration nectar of blazing colour and intergearing components. Isn't that enough?'

'I see,' Jonah said. Her love fell away from him like the flesh fizzing off of someone newly arrived in heaven. At that moment it seemed to him that she had circled his symptoms like a panther. She had convinced him that the world could be changed, not just commented upon. A child's fantasy: to adjust everything in one memorable outburst. 'Well. There it is. In that case I don't know what our consummation looks like. What happened with Tom?'

'Oh, I wanted to devour every atom of Tom, but he was a lover of men. The first time I saw him he had each strand of his hair decorated to a different theme. We consummated our love through revolution and the furious action of ideas. And it was magnificent. Our love was measured in a licking of flames. The most delicious excruciations. We ran across a field between fields. He was reckless for free. He could have a thousand eyes and not one to a profit. He lived like an explosion.'

'Well then. Should I retreat to my skull for old times' sake? Think myself back into a corner littered with numbers and needles? Spite from a distance, is it worth it? First I squandered my time in Babylon arranging my bloody bookshelves, stifled by this *ridiculous* mind and the certain knowledge that I'm an instalment of irrelevance. Every moment ran up the steps in front of me, making me flinch from all error until I was frozen in this world and its suspiciously tailor-made adversity. I somehow sat all day in a place the sun never came around to, until you walked into my basement. How could I know I'd make the acquaintance of a question that'd pull me up, start me on the spot, like I was begun there? But at this moment I'm sick of the taste of my own body. Why must I always be aboard? Taken where my body is? I'm ready to jump out my own throat, have done with it and admit the obvious.'

'Which is what exactly?'

'That my whole life has been lived specifically to cover my escape.'

'Oh Jonah, why die in a hurry? I'm the one carrying a bomb.'

'Independence, perhaps for the first time.'

She gave him a withering look. 'You're back to this, by the snap of my finger? A poor life, to be defeated by deference! Why do you care what I think?'

'I care how you feel, Sophie, and I think you relied on that. I was useless during the break-in. When that peeler turned up I started rattling on about a magic mouse in a storm. Really you had me there to embroil me.'

'Embroil!'

'Engross then. Absorb. I was in such a state of wonder and relief I didn't know how to say no.'

'Think, Jonah. Why set up an expensive radicalization programme when everyday adversity provides it all? At a certain point in a story – or an explanation – there is no going back. Its hooks are turned inward and it would kill you to remove it. So it is with life. It's too late to get out completely clean. We're meant to get dirty. If you see through everything you won't see anything. Don't be so impossible. And admit you became reckless with fascination. When such things start to happen it can be terrifying and wonderful. I don't want to unheart or unhead you, Jonah. I want you to claim it all and live in your soul! A ripe soul might burst its own skin!'

'You say it so casually. Are you really claiming to believe that truth is different depending on where you happen to be standing?'

'No. I believe we should stand where it can all be seen. Anything looks partial seen through a corner of someone else's context. And even the simplest true thing can look complicated from a complicated position. The assumption is that if it doesn't grow everywhere it isn't true. But life is so varied. It's funny isn't it, accepting only one facet? It's a round world. Tom gloried in difference like it was a cordial. Said it made him feel alive, or something like it. You've complained about how all of this, its substance and atmosphere, proceeds by the sickly peekaboo pretence that we aren't helpless. For you I'm referring to the honesty of helplessness, of giving up control. Acceptance as first position. In your case that may be a foundation, Jonah.'

Surprised, Jonah liked that very much. It rained in through a leaky ceiling. It was a truth the skull was meant to keep out.

'I understand the magic of a book,' Sophie continued. 'It falls through coiled centuries until we sit turning its ochre leaves. We speak across time by inhabiting the same autumn. But I tell you, for the mind that has already eaten more than it can use, the voice that escapes the head explains nothing, and there is more magic in the present cells of your body than in another's dusty book or sacred relic. Or some golden age. Even the Troy Jester said "I'll close your stale eyes in the freshness of rain." To feel a belonging in discovery is to live ongoing, in the moment. Truth. Eat it raw before it disappears, Jonah. My moody man.' Sophie kissed his mouth. Her teeth tasted of tea.

Jonah stood slowly like a new insect pulling out of its glue. His cleverness had closed so many wounds prematurely. Now they bled. Blazing trees, all sensitivity, fizzed like nerves. White pebbles sprouted under the wind. An old man with a woolly face sat seemingly bewildered, holding a penny farthing bicycle upright beside him. Jonah set off on the sort of walk where the previous step seemed an age ago. In the cracks in the pavement, old minutes. A worm flattened like a bootlace. Wallbills requesting connivance in the war. Shops as colourfully tasteless as antique candy. He moved through a party of crouching clowns and found himself crossing over the chocolate waters of the Fleet. Beyond was a disease of steeples. Ah, the looseness of being underway!

At the North shore, planks were showing through watery mud like ribs through rot. Dockers indulged in seaside gossip and nuns sat fishing off the jetty. Jonah started climbing the escapades, passing walls that looked like dirty nougat in the sinking sun. Halfway up he could see only a little scribble of horizon between two towers. Then he was in roofland, crossing galleys and gangways between buildings that seemed to bend the wrong way. Gargoyles had broiled in the weather, turning blunt and fossiliferous. Walls were scored with soot and vintage rust like gold. It was all becoming bathed in pink light. He could see a thin tower giving off convulving repetitions of influence, tamping down everything in the circle of its power. Down there were the Thousand Towers, all that remained of an earlier concept called a city. Accidental miracles fell loose into the hours. Jonah was undergoing sublime transactions on the roof of the world, an arterial goldrush in a place of utterly immense illumination. He was approaching something like the great flounced brain of a jellyfish. An angel came boiling past, blistering the walls and fizzing over his scalp. This was far from the old familiar whirlpool. Opening a sunburnt door, he found himself in a shimmering dimensional enclosure with veined diaphanous walls like the chamber of a shut flower. He ran his hands over a panel of pulsing gemstones. The entire structure pushed out into marvels new and complicated, blue gold plasmic matter torrenting past circular windows. He was drifting over infinite fields of snagged urgency, mazed with enamelled structures and bejewelled unnameable gadgets. It was a blissful complexity. He was headed toward a gobbling vortex.

And then all pageantry fell away, transfigured by one breath of fresh air. The town was ablaze.

22

The Tower

The basement door crawled open and Sophie crouched out, setting off up stairs of stone and steel, ascending the landlocked lighthouse that was Terminal Tower. At every storey the pink of sunset entered with more insistence. A couple of engineers in yellow protective gear collided with her, dashing away in panic down the stairs. Sophie entered what seemed to be a small canteen. From the opposite door former Lieutenant Lukas entered rather haphazardly, touching upon table and wall as though greeting old friends. He was wearing a ridiculous toytown uniform stained with gravy and vomit. He removed a bung from a hand-anker and poured something down his throat. Then his eyes focused upon her. She raised her veil.

'Sophie?'

'Oh Frank, what degradation is this now? Dressed as a fondant? Why do you abase yourself?'

His sweaty face glistened like a medal. 'Me? Well, it's a tricky matter.'

'Are you truly lost or just blotted out by others? Wasn't it enough to have your body and mind starved into the army?'

'Ah Sophie my love, you're a miracle for all the wrong reasons, like a bloody volcano. I should take you to Mr Brewster.'

'He's here in the building? Oh hell, Frank, take me.'

The round room at the summit was shifting with a strange crepuscular light – it was like being inside a magic lantern. Central to it was a large black structure, dense and delicate as the turbo of a poppy. This was crowned with a white radial array of needles. The contraption seemed to emanate a dismal fizz, less than grey, like a cloud of fast moths. Sophie felt a flux of pain in her head.

Brewster was standing at a spoked wheel like a ship's helm and spectating the city through a sweep of observation windows. He did not seem surprised to see her and was as jocular as ever. 'There she is, our valedictorian! My boon nemesis for the next few minutes! Here in the righteous name of liberation!'

'Ventilation,' she gulped. 'Fresh air of consequence.' But there was something in the air like the stink of bone-dust from a saw. Her eyes hurt as she looked at Brewster. She had never seen him so intensely. He seemed to have been hollowed out. Someone had worked to make an acute omission of the man. Though searingly unnatural, it was possible to be less than nothing, an ache without substance. Worse, he had done it to himself. A scrambling vacuum surrounded him and webbed the room's atmosphere like a migraine aura. Reaching for the knapsack, Sophie was buckling with nausea. Frank tried to support her.

'Bring her to the window, Middleman. Put the bag down there. You'll love this, Sophie. Take a look.'

Frank propped her at the window and she looked out onto an inferno. Torrential fire was cascading up the sides of towers, ingots of windows blinking in black walls. The fire was all one colour and the smoke seemed to come to a stop just above the towers, as though trapped in a glass box. Sophie glimpsed lines of influence criss-crossing the sky.

'It's tonight's stupid beano. All those backyard bonfires and town square auto-da-fes have joined together in a communal spirit, and the city's burning! Gone as far south as Bombley, I hear.'

'How did it cross the river?'

'On the number 7 bus, I believe. Fire – the first

lick opens, the second illuminates and the third burns away all that's unnecessary. Not really my plan but I can profit by anything, as you know. Oh my loyal collaborators! My dry suckers! I'm told it's a real hoot dying by fire, eh? Don't worry, this tower's reinforced, every stick of timber switched out. We have a little time. Put her in the chair, Middleman.'

Nestled within the amplifier was an oval metal seat riddled with wires. Frank dragged her over and strapped her inside, one of the silver bands going across her throat. He seemed exhausted by the effort and sank onto the floor looking into space, paws limp on his knees. Sophie could see Brewster moving against industrial complications, shuttling white levers and smiling imperviously. 'There'll be no knight come to rescue you, and Frank there is the cavalry. I've always liked the cut of your ears, young lady. The girl who knows better. A real cool traitor. I'm glad to have got a front row seat at your fruitless try. Frustration's a kind of power storage, a loop. For me you're a battery. What are you thinking now? I can see the cogs turning.'

'Long odds,' Sophie breathed, 'are very motivating.'

He stared at her as she twisted in the straps. 'You and me, beak-to-beak under a burnt sky. If you are the Rook, as I suspect, I want to thank you. I got my bearings by your failures three years in a row. Manufactured strife and appointed perdition. I keep a lid on it. Which of us is resisting the most, Sophie? Careful, it's a trick question. I live in the eye of the hoax. You have no idea how empty. A head like yours – certain it's right while excluding so much. That's the stuff! Now, there's no way I can prepare you for what's about to happen. Torture makes for a stout hour. Because you're young, you'll soon begin convulsing in the continental manner. It's an occasional treat for me. "Suppression in meaninglessness and the sour incandescence of its grinding abyss", how's that for a quote? I'll get ten volts out of you.'

'Get on with it. You bore me beyond endurance.'

Brewster tilted his head the way a fly does cleaning its eyes. 'Stop being so goddamn articulate! Scream like a baby! I'll scramble your soul yet!'

Sophie laughed. 'You can't handle my soul! I'll think till I blow up! I'm my own fucking Masada!'

'Your defence comprises of you being at stake. That's the stance of a martyr, a jamboree lamb! And you're dressed for a funeral!'

He looked aside and quickly raised his hand as if warding something off. A hole popped open in his palm.

§

Inspector Nightjar stood in the doorway with a smoking pistol in her hand. She was in her most complete suit of jet. She kept the gun raised, frowning at the sight of Sophie tangled insensible now amid the tin snarls of some giant resonator. Brewster was standing there, horribly empty, a thing and relieved to be so. He had situated himself at a point behind annihilation. Nightjar had the sudden impression of him as a blown egg, nothing but shell, the air around him aswarm with flurrying nothing. She felt very sick. It was far worse than the power station.

Brewster looked at his hand with a faintly puzzled expression. 'Criminal violence? On a Thursday? I thought you were a cop.'

'No, Mr Brewster, I'm very much alive.'

'I won't be the villain here.'

'Not your decision. And you're bleeding from the side of your neck. Release Miss Shafto from that newfangle and have a nice lie down.'

Brewster seemed bemused. 'Middleman,' he said, 'release the brat.'

The uniformed derelict on the floor roused himself from his sprawl like a dangly puppet. He dragged the silver bonds away from Sophie and hauled her clumsily into a heap beside the machine. She was beautiful. Perfect backbone, everything included. Nightjar bent to feel for her pulse.

Meanwhile the Middleman was crawling slowly like an infant out of the room. He seemed to be some kind of wind-up lackey, his duties dubious as those of a cabin boy. 'Huzzah!' Brewster called after him. 'Honour bright!'

'Now, Mr Brewster, make so bold as to sit in the goddamn seat.'

'I suppose I could right away, but –' Nightjar conferred her fist upon his face without ceremony, a distasteful business she could have done without. His skin felt like a rotten vegetable. He seemed less stunned than surprised. Nightjar pulled on her black gloves and set about propelling him toward the chrome chair. He danced along with her in a way that filled her with revulsion. He almost giggled. She bound the straps over his chest, trying to make as little contact with his flesh as possible, even through the gloves. 'When a man has less character than his collar,' she said, 'as you do, it makes me wonder. Yes, I wonder what occurs when a vacuum is sucked through a vacuum. My guess is you'll last about as long as a pinstripe bug in a blast furnace.' She stepped back from the scrambling grey air of the amplifier.

Sophie was recovering, standing unsteadily and surveying the scene.

'You two won't last much longer,' Brewster said. 'Connections will be spent into the dark. Things treasured unto death are flipped into the trash after. Hope's a cheap refuge from the future. The future, you know what I see? A factory long as a city. Proportions designed to annihilate the individual, while allowing them to manoeuvre in their clockwork petticoats or whatever the rebellious fad is, eh?'

'Get on and die,' Sophie gasped.

'She's right, really,' Nightjar added, 'is there no limit to your evasion?'

Brewster's skin was flaking like the paint off a fake pearl. 'Space is infinite, I'm told. I refuse to be diabolical, Inspector. My machines are infernal only in the true sense – power from restriction, too quiet to call much notice. Buy Amerikaana bonds.' Then he caved like an old cadaver, sucking into himself. Particulates of burnt dust swarmed the room.

Nightjar put her arm about Sophie, holding her upright. 'Bravo, brigand. But you're not too lofty to be rescued.'

'Is he dead?'

'It's hard to tell what's real in here. Come on, let's go.'

'Break the machine,' Sophie moaned, but Nightjar was already guiding her out of the control room.

Partway down the stairwell they found the Middleman sitting on a step, transfixed by the ferocious blaze and falling bits of fire outside the window. Then Nightjar realised he was watching an airship which was powering toward the tower at a rate of speed, and that a recognisable figure was at the tiller. It was that feeble librarian from Drood Street. He seemed to be in a trance of happiness.

They left the drunkard halfway up and halfway down, staring outward.

Emerging into the nitrous air, din and chaos of the burning city, ducking under a rain of sparks, they ran to a position in the middle of a street seemingly come undone and covered in sores. From here they witnessed the skywhale, its great engines straining as it stove into the top of Terminal Tower. The groaning airship burst its skin and released upward a glittering explosion of stars. Flames belted out of the tower's cavity and the amplifier's sickly seams of force flickered and disappeared.

'He did it,' Sophie gasped. 'That sweet juicy bastard did it.'

The smoke was free to rise and acidic bursts of grace flared across the city, bending waves of ferocious air into coronal arches. Every flame was a different colour and inflection. The horizon was confused with flying blots of light and rising streaks of vapour. A blush of elation flushed through everything.

'Look. The sky's falling upward.'

Rain began to fall as the smoke bent into jigsaw edges above the city, a universe weeping in all directions.

Sophie laughed. 'What a beautiful mess.'

Steve Aylett is author of *Lint, Slaughtermatic, Heart of the Original* and comics including *Hyperthick*.

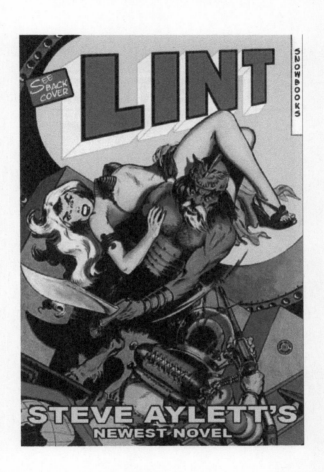

NOVAHEAD

"The most original and most consciousness-altering living writer in the English language, not to mention one of the funniest"
Alan Moore

STEVE AYLETT

Heart of the Original
STEVE AYLETT

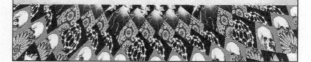

ORIGINALITY, CREATIVITY, INDIVIDUALITY

"A sizzling and hilarious manifesto where its author
means every blazing word" –ALAN MOORE

"A new dimension of poetic genius." —ALAN MOORE

TAO TE JINX

Steve Aylett

REBEL AT THE
END OF TIME

STEVE AYLETT

A NEW ADVENTURE IN MICHAEL MOORCOCK'S
'END OF TIME' UNIVERSE

'A terrific read'
THE FACE

SLAUGHTER
TER MATICS

STEVE AYLETT

THE COMPLETE
ACCOMPLICE

STEVE AYLETT

ONLY AN ALLIGATOR
THE VELOCITY GOSPEL
DUMMYLAND
KARLOFF'S CIRCUS

WITH AN INTRODUCTION BY
MICHAEL MOORCOCK

FAIN THE SORCERER

STEVE AYLETT